ROB BELL is the *New York Times* bestselling author of *Love Wins*, *What We Talk About When We Talk About God*, *The Zimzum of Love* and his most recent book *What Is the Bible?* iTunes named his podcast, *The Rob-Cast*, Best of 2015. He's been profiled in the *New Yorker*, he's toured with Oprah on her *Life You Want* tour and in 2011 TIME magazine named him one of the 100 Most Influential People in the World. He has a regular show at Largo, the legendary music and comedy club in West Hollywood. Rob and his wife, Kristen, have three children and live in Los Angeles.

'Inspired me to live life with a deeper appreciation and to love people with a greater awareness of our connectivity'
Aaron Rodgers, quarterback for
the Green Bay Packers

'Plenty of inspiration and provocation'
*Relevant Magazine*

'Engaging, accessible and engrossing'
*Englewood Review of Books*

**ALSO BY ROB BELL**

# How To Be Here

# HOW
# TO
# BE
# HERE

A Guide to Creating a Life
Worth Living

## ROB BELL

WILLIAM
COLLINS

HarperCollins
PUBLISHERS
Since 1817

William Collins
An imprint of HarperCollins*Publishers*
1 London Bridge Street
London SE1 9GF

www.WilliamCollinsBooks.com

First published in Great Britain by William Collins in 2016
First published in the United States by Harper One in 2016
This William Collins paperback edition published in 2017

1

Copyright © 2016 by WORB, Inc.

Rob Bell asserts the moral right to be identified as the author of this work

Designed by Joan Olson

A catalogue record for this book is available from the British Library

ISBN 978–0–00–759134–3

Printed and bound in Great Britain by Clays Ltd, St Ives plc

**MIX**
Paper from
responsible sources
FSC™ C007454

FSC™ is a non-profit international organisation established to promote
the responsible management of the world's forests. Products carrying the
FSC label are independently certified to assure consumers that they come
from forests that are managed to meet the social, economic and
ecological needs of present and future generations,
and other controlled sources.

Find out more about HarperCollins and the environment at
**www.harpercollins.co.uk/green**

# Contents

# PART 1

# The Blinking Line

*You are something the whole universe is doing in the same way that a wave is something that the whole ocean is doing.*

—Alan Watts

I once had an idea for a book.

I'd never written a book.

I was a pastor at the time and I'd been giving sermons week after week and I noticed that certain ideas and stories seemed to connect with people in a unique way. I began to see themes and threads and wondered whether I could bring them together to make something people would read and pass along to their friends. I already had a job, so I figured the only way to write a book was to hire a stenographer—the person who sits in a courtroom and records everything that is said during a trial—and speak the book out loud in one sitting while he typed what I said.

So that's what I did. I stood there in a room and I spoke the book out loud while KevinTheStenographer typed away. It took an entire day.

And it was awful. Seriously—it was so bad.

There was a moment in the middle of the afternoon when I was talking and suddenly I realized that I wasn't even listening to what I was saying. I had somehow managed to stop paying attention to *myself*.

A few days later Kevin sent me the typed manuscript of what I'd said and I started reading it, but it was like a mild form of torture. It just didn't work.

It was *my words,* but it wasn't *me,* if that makes sense.

All of which led me to the shocking realization that if I was going to write a book, *I was going to have to actually write a book.*

Which sounds obvious, but at the time it was a revelation.

I remember sitting down at my desk, opening up a new word-processing document, and staring at that blank page with that blinking line in the upper left-hand corner. I wasn't prepared for how intimidating it would be. *Other people are writers*—actual, you know, *authors.* And there are lots of them, many who have been doing it for years.

I thought about Christopher Moore's book about Biff the thirteenth disciple
and Annie Dillard's line about physics labs
and everything Nick Hornby has ever written
and Dorothy Sayers's words about Trinitarian creativity
and anything by Dave Eggers. . . .

I was now going to try and do *that*? The blinking line on that blank page kept blinking, like it was taunting me.

There's a reason it's called a *cursor*.

*We all have a blinking line.*

**Your blinking line is whatever sits in front of you waiting to be brought into existence.**

It's the book
or day
or job
or business
or family
or mission
or class
or plan
or cause
or meeting
or task
or project
or challenge
or phone call
or *life* that is waiting for you to bring it into being.

# An Unfinished World

Do you see your life as something you create?
Or do you see your life as something that is happening
to you?

The blinking line raises a compelling question:
*What are we here for?*

For many people, the world is already created.
It's a fixed, static reality—set in place, previously
established, done. Or to say it another way: *finished*.
Which usually leads to the question: *What's the point of
any of this?*

But when we're facing the blinking line and we talk
about bringing something new into existence, we're
expressing a different view of the world, one in which
the world is *unfinished*.

There's an ancient poem about this unfinished world we call home. In this poem there are stars and fish and earth and birds and animals and oceans, and they're all in the endless process of becoming. It's not just a tree, it's a tree that produces fruit that contains seeds that will eventually grow new trees that will produce new fruit that contains more seeds to make more new trees. It's a world exploding with life and beauty and complexity and diversity, all of it making more, becoming and evolving in such a way that tomorrow will be different from today because it's all headed somewhere. Nothing is set in stone or static here; the whole thing is in motion, flush with vitality and pulsing with creative energy. (This poem, by the way, is the first chapter of the Bible, in case any of this is starting to sound familiar.)

And then, right there in the middle of all of this unfinished creation, the poet tells us about a man and a woman. The man's name is Adam, which means *The Human* in the original Hebrew language. It's not a common name like you and I have, it's more like a generic description. Same with the woman, whose name is Eve, which means *Source of Life* or *Mother of the Living.*

They find themselves in the midst of this big, beautiful, exotic, heartbreaking, mysterious, endlessly becoming, unfinished world and they're essentially told,

*Do something with it!*
*Make something!*
*Take it somewhere!*
*Enjoy it!*

The poet wants us to know that God is looking for partners, people to help co-create the world. To turn this story into a debate about whether or not Adam and Eve were real people or to read this poem as a science textbook is to miss the provocative, pointed, loaded questions that the poem asks:

*What will Adam and Eve do with this extraordinary opportunity?*
*What kind of world will they help make?*
*Where will they take it?*
*What will they do with all this creative power they've been given?*

It's a poem about them, but it asks questions about all of us:

*What will we make of our lives?*
*What will we do with our energies?*
*What kind of world will we create?*

Which leads to the penetrating question for every one of us—including you:

*What will you do with your blinking line?*

# Ex Nihilo-ness

**You create your life.**

You get to shape it, form it, steer it, make it into something. And you have way more power to do this than you realize.

**What you do with your life is fundamentally creative work.** The kind of life you lead, what you do with your time, how you spend your energies—it's all part of how you create your life.

**All work is ultimately creative work because all of us are taking part in the ongoing creation of the world.**

There's a great Latin phrase that helps me make sense of the wonder and weirdness of creating a life. *Ex nihilo* means *out of nothing*. I love this phrase because *you* didn't used to be here. And I wasn't here either. We didn't used to be here. And then we were here. We were conceived, we were birthed, we arrived.

Out of nothing came . . . us.
You.
Me.
All of us.
All of it.

There is an *ex nihilo-ness* to everything, and that includes each of us.

Who of us can make sense of our own existence?

Have you ever heard an answer to the question *How did we get here?* that even remotely satisfied your curiosity? (Is this why kids shudder when they think of their parents having sex? Because we get here through some very mysterious and unpredictable biological phenomena involving swimming and winning? . . . Our very origins are shrouded in strangeness. You and I are here, but we were almost *not* here.)

My friend Carlton writes and produces television shows and sometimes I watch his shows and I'll say to him, *How did you come up with that? Where did that come from?* We'll be laughing and I'll say, *What is going on inside your head that you can make this stuff up?*

Have you ever encountered something that another human being made and thought, *How did she do that? Where did that come from?*

When I was in high school my neighbor Tad, the drummer for the band Puddle Slug (they later changed their name to Rusty Kleenex to, you know, appeal to a wider audience) gave me two ceramic heads that he had made. One head is green and has a smiling face, and the other head is brown and has a frowning face. They are very odd sculptures. But at the time he gave them to me I was mesmerized.

You can do that?
You can take a pile of clay and break it in two and then mold it and work with it and make *that*?

As a seventeen-year-old I was flabbergasted with the *ex nihilo-ness* of what Tad had made.

He just sat down and came up with that?

(By the way, he gave them to me in 1988. I still have them; they're on the wall next to the desk where I'm writing this book. Twenty-eight years later.)

The *ex nihilo-ness* of art and design and music and odd sculptures and bizarre television shows reminds us of the *ex nihilo-ness* of our *lives*—we come out of nothing. And we're here. And we get to make something with what we've been given.

Which takes us back to this creation poem, which grounds all creativity in the questions that are asked of all of us:

*What kind of world are we making?*

Which always leads to the pressing personal question:

*What kind of life am I creating?*

# Accountants and Moms

Now for some of us, the moment we hear the word *create*, our first thought is,

*But you don't understand, I'm not the creative type*

or

*That's fine for some people, but I'm an accountant and it's just not that exciting*

or

*What does any of this have to do with being a mom?*

About ten years ago I was speaking at a conference and I decided to sit in the audience and listen to the speaker who spoke before me. He began his talk by saying that there are two types of people in the world: *numbers* people and *art* people. He explained that some people are born with creativity in their blood and so they do creative work and some people aren't—they're the numbers people—and that's fine because they can do other things.

I sat there listening, thinking, *That's total rubbish.*

Take accountants, for example.

Accountants work with numbers and columns and facts and figures and spreadsheets. Their job is to keep track of what's being made and where it's going and how much is available to make more. That structure is absolutely necessary for whatever is being done to move forward. It is a fundamentally creative act to make sure things have the shape and form and internal coherence they need.

Obviously, bureaucracies and institutions and governments and finance departments can be huge obstacles to doing compelling work, but ideally—*in spirit*—the person who gives things their much needed structure and order is playing a vital role in the ongoing creation of the world, helping things move forward. (Which is an excellent litmus test for whether the work you're doing is work that the world needs: Does it move things forward? Because some work doesn't. Some work takes things in the wrong direction. Some things people give their energies to prevent other people from thriving. Some tasks dehumanize and degrade the people involved. Perhaps you're in one of those jobs, the kind that sucks the life out of your soul and you can't see the good in it. Stop. Leave. Life is too short to help make a world you don't want to live in.)

And then there are moms. I've met moms who say *I'm just a mom . . .*

*Just a mom?*
*What!?*

Could anything be more connected to the ongoing creation of the world than literally, physically bringing new human beings into existence and then nurturing that new life as it's shaped and formed?

All work is creative work because all work is participating in the ongoing creation of the world.

# Suffering

But what about the things that happen to us that we never wanted to happen? What about tragedy and loss and heartbreak and illness and abuse—that list can be long.

What about all of the things that come our way that make us feel powerless and out of control, like our life is being created for us?

When I was growing up, my dad would come into my room every night before I went to bed and tell me that he loved me, and then he would stand in the doorway before he turned out the light and he would say, *You're my pride and joy.* He coached my soccer and basketball teams, he took us on vacations, he made my sister and brother and me pancakes on Saturday mornings, he helped us with our homework. When I left home to go to college, he sent me handwritten letters every week, never failing to remind me that he was cheering me on.

I tell you about how present and involved my dad was in my life growing up because when he was eight, his uncle picked him up at his house to take him somewhere. His cousin was in the backseat of the car, and when my dad asked his cousin where they were going, his cousin said, *To the funeral home—don't you know? Your dad died.*

That's how he found out his dad had died: from his cousin in the backseat of a car on the way to the funeral home. His dad, whom he hadn't known very well because his dad was gone during the war, had cancer and died at age thirty-four.

When my dad was fifteen, his mother became very sick, and he and his brother thought she was going to die. He once told me that while his mother was in the hospital, his brother clung to him through the night, repeating over and over with terror in his voice, *Are we going to be all alone in the world?*

She eventually recovered, but then a year later my dad's brother, who was his best friend and constant companion, died unexpectedly in an accident.

How does a person bear that kind of pain?
How does a heart ever recover?
How does a young man make his way in the world when he's experienced that much suffering?

Somewhere in the midst of all that pain and loss, my dad decided that someday he would have a family and he would be the father that he had always wished he had. And so that's what he did.

**How we respond to what happens to us—especially the painful, excruciating things that we never wanted and we have no control over—is a creative act.**

Who starts cancer foundations? Usually people who have lost a loved one to cancer.
Who organizes recovery groups? Mostly people who have struggled with addiction.
Who stands up for the rights of the oppressed? Often people who have experienced oppression themselves.

We have power, more power than we realize, power to decide that we are going to make something good out of *even this* . . .

There's a question that you can ask about the things that have come your way that you didn't want. It's a question rooted in a proper understanding of the world, a question we have to ask ourselves continually throughout our lives:

*What new and good thing is going to come out of even this?*

When you ask this question, you have taken something that was out of your control and reframed it as another opportunity to take part in the ongoing creation of the world.

Death. Disease. Disaster. Whatever it is, you will have to grieve it. And maybe be angry about it. Or be in shock. Or shake your fists at the heavens for the injustice of it.

That's normal and healthy and often needed.

But then, as you move through it, as time does its healing work, you begin to look for how *even this* has potential. Even this is a blinking line.

# Breath

I once watched a doctor hold my newborn son upside down by the ankles and give him a shake.

I was shocked.
*What?* You can do that to a baby?

Because up until that moment I was under the impression that babies were incredibly fragile, like a high-grade combination of porcelain and glass. But the doctor handled him when he first entered the world like he was made of rubber. He did this, I quickly learned, for a very specific reason: He was trying to help my son take his first breath. Because if you don't take a breath in those first few seconds when you arrive, you have a very serious problem.

And so my boy in all his shiny pink glory hung there, upside down, with strange liquids exiting his various orifices, and then he coughed and gasped and took his first breath.

Remembering that day takes me to another day, this one a decade later. It was a Friday night, August 22, 2008, and my family and I were visiting my grandma Eileen. My grandma and I had been great friends since I was young. When I was in my late twenties and early thirties, she and I had lunch together every Friday *for a decade*. We, as they say, *rolled deep*.

But when we went to visit her that evening in August, everything was different. She was in her mid-eighties and her health had been declining over the past year and she'd been moved to a different part of the nursing home where she lived. We knew we were getting close to the end, but I still wasn't expecting what we experienced when we entered her room. She was lying in bed, her eyes closed, taking long, slow breaths, but something about her was absent.

It was like she was in the room, but not in the room. Here, but already gone.

If you've ever been in the room with someone who is dying, you know exactly what I'm talking about. There's a physical body right there in front of you, but something's missing. Spirit, soul, presence, essence— whatever words you use for it, there's a startling vacancy you feel in being with someone you've been with so many times before and yet that person isn't there anymore.

I froze in the doorway, watching her lying on the bed, as it began to sink in that she was at the end of her life. You know someone is going to die because you know we're all going to die—you know it in your brain. But then there's a moment when that truth drops from your brain to your heart, like an elevator in free fall, and lands with a thud.

My wife Kristen, however, walked right over to the bed, sat down next to Grandma, took Grandma's hands in her own, and leaned in over her heart and began to speak to her:

*Grandma, we're here with you now. We see that you're going to be leaving us soon. We love you and we have loved being with you all these years and now we're letting you go . . .*

It was so moving.

We spent a few hours with Grandma that evening, and then we left and within a few hours she died.

There is a moment when you arrive and you take your first breath, and then there is a moment when you take your last breath and you leave.

For thousands of years humans have been aware that our lives intimately and ultimately depend on our breath, which is a physical reflection of a deeper, unseen reality. It isn't just breath we're each given—it's life itself.

Before anything else can be said about you, you have received a gift. God / the universe / ultimate reality / being itself—whatever word you want to use for source—has given you life.

Are you breathing?
Are you here?
Did you just take a breath?
Are you about to take another?
Do you have a habit of regularly doing this?
Gift.
Gift.
Gift.

Whatever else has happened in your life—failure, pain, heartache, abuse, loss—the first thing that can be said about you is that you have received a gift.

Often you'll meet people who have long lists of ways they've been slighted, reasons the universe has been unfair to them, times they got the short end of the stick or were dealt a bad hand of cards.

While we grieve and feel and lament and express whatever it is that is brewing within us, a truth courses through the veins of all our bumps and bruises, and it is this: We have received.

You're here,
you're breathing,
and you have received a gift,
a generous, extraordinary, mysterious, inexplicable
gift.

# Alert and Awake

I once visited a man named John who was dying of cancer. I'd never met him before, but a mutual friend had asked me to see him at his house. He was lying in a hospital bed in his living room when I came in, his body frail and ravaged. And yet his eyes were clear and full of shimmering life. After we shook hands and I sat down, he told me,

*People just don't get it*

as he smiled and then repeated,

*People just don't get it.*

He said that phrase over and over and over again for the next hour, in between bursts of conversation. When I asked him what he meant by it, he said that people don't understand how precious and incredible life is. He said he hadn't understood this truth until he knew that it was being taken from him.

Because that's how it works, doesn't it?

**Suffering and loss have this extraordinary capacity to alert and awaken us to the gift that life is.**

You're driving down the road arguing with someone you love about something stupid when a car almost runs you off the road—and suddenly your hearts are pounding as you turn to each other and say, *That was close!* And you aren't arguing anymore.

You're frustrated with your kid and then you hear about someone else's kid being in the hospital, and when you get home you hold your kid extra close.

You go to a funeral and you sit there grieving the death of this person you loved but when you leave you realize that mixed in with your sadness is a strange sort of energy that comes from a renewed awareness that you're here and this is your life and it's good and it's a sacred gift.

Why do we react in these ways? Because deep down we know that all we have is a gift.

Jesus taught his disciples a prayer that begins,

*Our father, who's in heaven . . .*

. . . which is another way of saying,

*Begin your prayers—begin your day—by acknowledging that your life is a gift and this gift flows from a source. This source is responsible for the air in your lungs, the blood that courses through your veins, and the vitality that surges through you and everything around you.*

. . . which is another way of saying,

*Begin whatever you're doing by remembering that you are here and you have been given a gift.*

The blinking line reminds you that whatever has happened to you, whatever has come your way that you didn't want, whatever you have been through, you have *today*, you have *this moment*, you have a life that you get to create. The universe is unfinished, and God is looking for partners in the ongoing creation of the world.

# Bored

Boredom is lethal. Boredom says, *There's nothing interesting to make here*. Boredom reveals what we believe about the kind of world we're living in. Boredom is lethal because it reflects a static, fixed view of the world—a world that is finished.

Cynicism is slightly different from boredom, but just as lethal. Cynicism says, *There's nothing new to make here*. Often, cynicism presents itself as wisdom, but it usually comes from a wound. Cynicism acts as though it's seen a lot and knows how the world works, shooting down new ideas and efforts as childish and uninformed. Cynicism points out all the ways something could go wrong, how stupid it is, and what a waste of time it would be. Cynicism holds things at a distance, analyzing and mocking and noting all the possibilities for failure. Often, this is because the cynic did try something new at some point and it went belly up, he was booed off the stage, and that pain causes him to critique and ridicule because there aren't any risks in doing that. If you hold something at a distance and make fun of it, then it can't hurt you.

And then there's despair. While boredom can be fairly subtle and cynicism can appear quite intelligent and even funny, despair is like a dull thud in the heart. Despair says, *Nothing that we make matters*. Despair reflects a pervasive dread that it's all pointless and that we are, in the end, simply wasting our time.

Boredom, cynicism, and despair are spiritual diseases because they disconnect us from the most primal truth about ourselves—that we are here.

All three distance us from and deaden us to the questions the blinking line asks:
*How are you going to respond to this life you have been given?*
*What are you going to do with it?*
*What are you going to make here?*

# PART 2

# The Blank Page

*What you know makes you unique in some other way. Be brave. Map the enemy's positions, come back, tell us all you know. And remember that plumbers in space is not such a bad setup for a story.*

—**Stephen King**

I once had an idea for a book called *Fire in the Wine*.

I had a big black sketchbook on my shelf and I had this insight about the human body and soil and the food we eat and how when we die we're buried in the earth, which is what we do with seeds that then grow into the food that we consume that sustains our bodies that will be buried when we die . . . so I made a drawing to represent all of that.

It was just one sketch.

And then a few months later I came across a quote which somehow connected with that drawing that I had copied on the next page of that big black sketchbook.

And then something happened to me that reminded me of that first sketch and that quote which connected to something I'd read in a magazine around that time.

This continued for several years until I could see a book emerging on the pages of that sketchbook, a book I decided to call *Fire in the Wine*. As I began to organize the content of *Fire in the Wine* into chapters

I realized that I needed to do some reading to give more breadth and depth to the ideas I was working on. So I read. And read. And read. Thousands of pages. And whenever I came across something that spurred a thought or clarified something I'd been thinking about, I underlined it or marked the page. I then went back through those books and took notes on what I'd underlined, copying each idea onto a 3×5 card.

Which took months.

I then laid all those cards out on the floor and looked for patterns and connections and common threads. There were a lot of those cards, and so just out of curiosity I started counting them. I lost track somewhere past six hundred.

Once the cards were organized, I started writing the book, crafting the chapters, creating the introduction, working on the first draft.

Which took months.

I turned in that first draft to my editor, who visited me a few weeks later to talk about the book—the book that, he informed me, didn't appear to have a clear point.

I then rearranged the entire thing, moving the start to the end and the end to the beginning.

Which took months.

Months in which it became clear that the book wasn't really about fire in the wine, it was about something else. I kept using a phrase that I didn't realize I was repeating until my editor pointed it out. That phrase seemed like it should be the title of the book, so I changed the name of the book. Changing the name then shifted some of the central themes, which meant I had to go back through and rearrange the entire book, moving the quantum physics part to the beginning and organizing the rest of the book around seven central themes.

Which took months.

By the fifth draft, I had lost my way. I couldn't figure out how to take all that content and make it flow. It was like I had all the notes but no melody. I'd sit there and stare at the computer screen for hours, trying to figure out how to make it flow.

Some days I'd write one new sentence.
One.
Other days I'd write one new sentence, and then, at the end of the day, *I'd delete that one sentence.*

Many, many mornings—by this point well over a year of mornings—I'd get up and make my kids breakfast and take them to school and then I'd sit down at my desk and go through the book AGAIN, looking for even the slightest bit of help to find a way forward.

And that's when the head games started. You know about head games—those voices in your head, questioning who you are and what you're doing. Telling you you're no good.

This was the sixth book I'd written, so you'd think it wouldn't have been so hard. But it was. It was the most difficult thing I'd ever made. It didn't matter that I'd done it before. It didn't matter that I'd done months and months of outlining and arranging. It didn't matter that I cared deeply about the content.

The blinking line can be brutal.

Because the blinking line doesn't just taunt you with all the possibilities that are before you, the potential, all that you sense could exist but isn't yet because you haven't created it. The blinking line also asks a question:

*Who are you to do this?*

And that question can be paralyzing. It can prevent us from overcoming inertia. It can cause crippling doubt and stress. It can keep us stuck on the couch while life passes us by.

# Out of Your Head

To answer the question, *Who are you to do this?*,

**you first have to get out of your head.**

I use this phrase *out of your head* because that's where it's easy to get stuck. Somewhere between our hearts and our minds is an internal dialogue, a running commentary on what we think and feel and believe. It's the voices in your head that speak doubt and insecurity and fear and anxiety. Like a tape that's jammed on "repeat," these destructive messages will drain an extraordinary amount of your energies if you aren't clear and focused and grounded.

To get out of your head, it's important to embrace several truths about yourself and those around you, beginning with this one:

### Who you aren't isn't interesting.

You have a list of all the things you aren't, the things you can't do, the things you've tried that didn't go well. Regrets, mistakes that haunt you, moments when you crawled home in humiliation. For many of us, this list is the source of a number of head games, usually involving the words,

*Not _____ enough.*

Not smart enough,
not talented enough,
not disciplined enough,
not educated enough,
not beautiful, thin, popular, or hardworking enough,

you can fill in the _____.

Here is the truth about those messages:
### They aren't interesting.

What you haven't done,
where you didn't go to school,
what you haven't accomplished,
who you don't know and what you are scared of

*simply aren't interesting.*

I'm not very good at math. If I get too many numbers in front of me I start to space out.

See? Not interesting.

If you focus on who you aren't, and what you don't
have, or where you haven't been, or skills or talents
or tools or resources you're convinced aren't yours,
precious energy will slip through your fingers that you
could use to do something with that blinking line.

In the same way that who you *aren't* isn't interesting
when it comes to getting out of your head,

**who "they" are isn't interesting.**

We all have our *they*—friends, neighbors, co-workers,
family members, superstars who appear to skate by
effortlessly while we slog it out. *They* are the people we
fixate on, constantly holding their lives up to our life,
using their apparent ease and success as an excuse to
hold back from doing our work and pursuing our path
in the world.

Siblings who don't have to study and still get better
grades. Brothers-in-law who make more money
without appearing to work very hard. Friends who
have kids the same age as ours and yet they never
seem stressed or tired and always look great.

There's a moving moment in one of the accounts
of Jesus's life where he's reunited with one of his
disciples, a man named Peter. (I started out as a
preacher, and so these stories are in my blood.) Peter
is the disciple who had denied that he even knew
Jesus earlier in the story, and you can feel his relief

when Jesus forgives him, telling him he has work for Peter to do.

And how does Peter respond to this powerful moment of reconciliation?

He points to one of Jesus's other disciples and asks, *What about him?*

All Peter can think about is *someone else's path*. He's with Jesus, having a conversation, and yet his mind is *over there*, wondering about John.

Peter asks,
*What about him?*
and Jesus responds,
*What is that to you?*

# Comparisons

In the movie *Comedian,* Jerry Seinfeld runs into a young comedian named Orny Adams backstage at a club where they are both performing and Orny says to him,

"You get to a point where you're like 'How much longer can I take it?'"

Jerry is utterly perplexed by Orny's sentiment, asking, "What—is time running out?"

Orny then begins a litany of complaints and excuses— "I'm getting older. . . . I feel like I've sacrificed so much of my life."

Jerry is amazed, "Is there something else you would rather have been doing? Other appointments or places you gotta be?"

Then Orny pulls out a new line of complaints: "I see my friends are making a lot of money. . . . Did you ever stop and compare your life? Okay, I'm twenty-nine and my friends are all married and they all have kids and houses. They have some sort of sense of normality. What do you tell your parents?"

Jerry's response: "Are you out of your mind? . . . This has nothing to do with your friends. It's such a special thing. This has nothing to do with making it."

I love those lines from Seinfeld:
*This has nothing to do with your friends.*
*It's such a special thing.*
*This has nothing to do with making it.*

**Decide now that you will not spend your precious energy speculating about someone else's life and how it compares with yours.**

We each have our own life, our own blinking line, and every path has its own highs and lows, ups and downs, joys, challenges, and difficulties.

When you compare yourself with others, you have no idea what challenges they are facing.

Bruce Springsteen struggled for years with depression. What? The Boss? His shows are three hours long, leaving everybody wondering, *How does he do that?* Bruce Springsteen, who seems to never run out of energy, who's thriving more than ever in his sixties?

Yes. The Boss has had his struggles. Everybody does.

**We rob ourselves of immeasurable joy when we compare what we do know about ourselves with what we don't know about someone else.**

You have your life.
And your life is not her life. Or his life.
And his life is not yours,
and neither is hers.

Is there any way in which you've been asking,
*What about them?*
when the better question is,
*What is that to you?*

There will always be someone who's smarter than you.
There will always be someone with more raw talent than you.
There will always be someone more experienced and better qualified and harder working and stronger and more articulate and more creative with more stamina who can sing better than you can.

But who you *aren't* isn't interesting.

And who *they are* isn't interesting when it comes to who you are and what your path is.

# The You Experiment

That question the blinking line asks,
*Who are you to do this?*
can keep you locked up for years, living in fear and
doubt, looking over your fence or your shoulder,
comparing yourself with the people around you.

But the first word about you is gift,
and you're here and you're breathing,
and you get to take part in the ongoing creation of
the world. Creation is exhausting and exhilarating
and draining and invigorating and it's also a mystery
because

**everybody sits down to a blank page.**

Or business plan.
Or test or experiment or meeting or deal.
Or child or job or life.

Especially those who have done it before.

The more you do the work, the more you build muscles for that particular work. From shaping metal to forming paragraphs to arguing a case to doing research to making spreadsheets to arranging the parts for the violins to play to organizing staff to raising a child—you can acquire skills and then improve on them as you do the work year after year. This growing technique and expertise can help you create and build and act with more ease and excellence, but it cannot help you avoid the blank page.

This is true for rocket scientists and actors and doctors, and it's also true for parents and for people who work in restaurants and for your insurance agent.

**Whoever you are and whatever work you do, no one has ever lived your life with your particular challenges and possibilities.**

No one has ever raised that child before, even if you've raised two already.

No one has ever worked in that particular office before with its peculiar mix of personalities and challenges.

No one has ever taken care of that patient at this moment with these particular challenges.

*"You" hasn't been attempted before.*

It can be intimidating when you look around and see the superstars in whatever field you're in doing their thing. You see the tremendous momentum they gain from success after success and it can easily plant the question in your heart, *Why should I even try?*

Or you can see it another way.

**It can be intimidating, or it can be liberating, because if everybody starts with a blank page, then everybody starts from the same place.**

This is the great mystery of creation: something comes out of nothing. Whatever it is—a school, a business, a treatment program, a sculpture, a network, a family, a relationship, a strategy—it didn't exist, and then it did exist, because someone brought it into existence.

When you say "yes" to your life and your path and your work in the world, you are entering into this mystery of creation, a mystery in which **everybody starts with a blank page,** and "everybody" includes you.

Now, let's pause and take a breath.
You've been given this gift of life.

You were not given *his* gift or *her* gift.
You were given *your* gift.

Is there any way that you've been looking over your shoulder or over your fence, comparing your life with someone else's?

Is there any way in which you wish you had someone else's life?

Is there any way in which you are not throwing yourself into your life because you're convinced that you could never do it as well as so-and-so does it?

Is there any way in which the blank page that is your life has got you stuck, terrified, asking that soul-crushing question,

*Who am I to do this?*

There is a new question,
a better question,
a question that will help you to be *here*.

The new question is this:
**Who am I not to do this?**
(Who *am'n't* I?)

# PART 3

# The Japanese Have a Word for It

*You may be talented, but you're not Kanye West.*

—Kanye West

I once volunteered to give a sermon.

I'd never given a sermon. How do you put together a sermon? I had no idea. I took a walk to think about it and had a few ideas, so I wrote them down. A few more thoughts came the next day, so I wrote them down. I read some passages in the Bible, which spurred some more thoughts, so I wrote them down.

And then Sunday morning came and I stood up to speak. I clearly remember standing there about to start my talk and knowing that this was what I was going to do with my life.

It wasn't just the speaking part that I loved, it was the preparation and the nerves and arranging the ideas and going over it again and again, trying to make it better—I loved everything leading up to giving that sermon. I loved the whole process.

There's another memory I have of that morning that's mixed in among the trembling nerves and explosive joy, one that hasn't left me twenty-five years later. I specifically remember thinking that even if I wasn't very good at giving sermons, I had found something that would get me out of bed in the morning . . .

The Japanese have a word for what gets you out of bed in the morning: they call it your *ikigai*. Your ikigai is that sense you have when you wake up that this day matters, that there are new experiences to be had, that you have work to do, a contribution to make. Sometimes this is referred to as your calling, other times your vocation, your destiny, your path. Your ikigai is your reason for being.

If you're like a lot of people, the moment the words *path* and *vocation* and *calling* come into the conversation, let alone a new word like *ikigai,* a thousand questions come to mind. Questions about paychecks and responsibility and passion and what you wish you could do if only you didn't have those bills to pay . . .

# Figuring It Out

We are always in the endless process of figuring out our ikigai.

Your ikigai is a web of work and family and play and how you spend your time,
what you give your energies to,
what you say "yes" to,
what you say "no" to,
what new challenges you take on,
things that come your way that you never wanted or planned for or know what to do with—

your ikigai is a work in progress because you are a work in progress.

Knowing your ikigai, then, takes patience,
and insight,

and courage,
and honesty.

You try lots of different things. You volunteer, you
sign up, you take a class, you do an internship, you get
the training, you shadow someone around for a day
who does something that intrigues you. You follow
your curiosity. You watch for things that grab your
attention. This is much easier when you're younger
and have less financial pressure and fewer others
depending on you, but it's true no matter how old
you are.

**You explore the possibilities because you can't steer
a parked car.**

The one thing that unites the people I know who are
on satisfying and meaningful paths is that they kept
trying things, kept exploring, kept pursuing new
opportunities, kept searching until they discovered
their ikigai. And then from there they never stop
figuring it out because they understand how absolutely
crucial this is in creating a life worth living.

# Someone Should

When you pursue your path, exploring the possibilities as you search for your ikigai, pay careful attention to things that make you angry and get you all riled up and provoke you to say, *Someone should do something about that!!!*

**The someone may be you.**

When I was growing up, my parents took us to church. At church, I heard stories about Jesus. I loved those stories. I loved how Jesus always went to the edges, to the forgotten, to the outcasts, to those on the underside. I love how he answered questions with more questions, constantly challenging authority. I loved that he was funny and serious and shocking and irreverent and compelling all at the same time. I found him fascinating and compelling. I believed.

But there was this whole thing surrounding him—not just church, but a system that had built up around him of assumptions and rules and worldviews that appeared to me to have nothing to do with his life and message.

Why was he so thrilling but the religion that had organized around him so boring and oppressive?

I realize now, looking back many years later, that seeds were being planted in those early years. Seeds that would grow over time into my ikigai.

Some people find their ikigai by asking, *What do I love to do?*

Others find theirs by asking, *What makes me angry? What wrongs need to be righted? What injustice needs to be resisted?*

Listen to your life. Look back on the moments when you felt most connected to the world around you. Think about those experiences in which you felt the most comfortable in your own skin. Reflect on when you were most aware of something wrong in the world and your strong response to it.

Be honest about your joy. Sometimes our ikigai is jammed way down in our hearts somewhere because we were told early on, *You can't make money doing that,* or *That isn't a real job,* or *That's a waste of time.*

Ask yourself: *Am I not pursuing my path because of what someone has told me is and isn't acceptable?*

Which leads to another truth about your ikigai: **It may involve a paycheck and it may not.**

I once recorded an album that no one cared about.

I had written a number of songs so I booked time at a studio near my house, but I didn't have a band at the time so I had a friend play the drums and I played everything else. I had it mixed and mastered and I made a few copies for friends.

Who didn't say a thing.

Literally, I would play them the songs and when each song was done they'd say something like, *I heard it's supposed to rain later this week,* or *Didn't you say you had some queso dip you'd made? I'd love to try it . . .*

Quite quickly I realized that no one cared about my music but me. Which was awkward at first, and then freeing.

**Some things you do for you.**

You do them because it gives you great satisfaction and it puts a smile on your face and that's it.

And that's fine.

It's not just fine, it's necessary. It makes you a better person, it fills your soul, it opens you up to life in its fullness.

So don't apologize for it, enjoy it.

You may love doing or creating or making or organizing something, but that's different from it being your job. If music was my job, I'd hate it. What often happens is that we love doing a particular thing and so our next thought is, *I should do this for my job.*

Here's the problem with that impulse: **Getting a paycheck for doing that thing you love may actually ruin it.**

I've met a number of people who are working at a particular job but they have this other passion/cause/ hobby that they love and they're convinced that if they could just quit that job and do _____ full time they would be much more fulfilled.

But it's not always true. If they quit that job and did _____ all day they might be miserable.

There's a chance that putting the weight and pressure of a paycheck on that thing you love might burden it with a load it can't bear.

Interests, art forms, talents, hobbies, missions, passions, service projects, and causes all have their proper place in our lives.

Some people have a mission, a cause, a love, a thing they're most passionate about—and it's not their job. What they need is a job that doesn't drain them, so that they'll have the energy they need for the thing they know they're here to do.

**There are lots of ways your ikigai will get worked out in your life.**

Some things we do fill us with life so that we can give ourselves to our work in the world with greater love and vitality and passion. Some things we get paid for, some things we don't.

**There's a good chance your ikigai will change over time.**

Relax, this is normal.

You may get trained to do one thing but end up doing something very different.

You may get your dream job and then get fired.

Or the company may have to lay people off or there's only one opportunity at the moment in that particular line of work and it's in New Zealand. Or Bangladesh. Or Ohio.

Someone you love may get sick and need you to care for her, you may have a child with special needs whose primary care falls to you, you may become injured and not be able to do that thing that you've done all these years.

That may happen.

And it's okay.

It's all part of how your ikigai gets worked out over the course of your life.

# Step

Several years ago I was talking with a very wealthy man I know—let's call him Wayne. Wayne doesn't have to work another day in his life. That kind of wealth. And yet all he wanted to talk about is how bored he is.

It's the *inertia of options*: If you don't have to go anywhere or do anything in the morning, that's what may happen. You may not go anywhere or do anything.

Wealth often ruins people, because having too many options can easily lead to being stuck, disconnected from your life because there's no pressing need to do anything.

As it's written in the book of Genesis, we make our way in the world by the sweat of our brow. Too much money, not enough money, too many demands, not enough challenge, stressed from all the responsibility,

bored and restless and ready for more responsibility—
there is a tension at the heart of our humanity that
none of us can escape.

**To be here is to embrace the spiritual challenge of
your ikigai, doing the hard work of figuring out who
you are and what you have to give the world.**

This is work we all have to do,
because we're all a piece of work,
in the endless process of exploring our ikigai.

I get up in the morning and I sit down and start
working on my next book or talk or show because it's
the most natural thing to do
*and yet*
it regularly takes all of the discipline and focus I can
possibly muster to stay here at this desk and keep
working.

I can't imagine being anywhere else
*and yet*
some days I can't imagine anything more difficult
than. the. next. sentence.

**Your ikigai is exhausting and exhilarating, draining
and invigorating, all at the same time.**

**There are moments when nothing in the world
seems more difficult, and yet you can't imagine doing
anything else.**

**There is a paradox to your ikigai because sometimes the easiest thing to do and the hardest thing to do will be the exact same thing.**

Selling your house, giving away possessions,
working multiple jobs for a period of time,
going back to school and moving in with friends or relatives,
sharing a car with your partner and riding your bike more,
investing all your savings in a new venture,
living on the other side of the world for a year—
your friends may not understand,
your co-workers may not get it,
your extended family may think you've lost your mind—
that's okay.

Better to receive some odd looks and have a few people roll their eyes than spend your days wondering,
*What if I did that . . . ?*
Take that step.
Make that leap.
Try that new thing.
If it helps clarify your ikigai,
if it gets you up in the morning,
if it's good for you and the world,
do it.

# Courage

So I preached that first sermon, and then later that year I went to seminary. And then I got a job in a church, and then I started giving sermons every week. And then I started traveling and speaking and writing books and then I made a television show and then I started a podcast—all of it one long, slow evolution in the same direction.

This work has brought me more joy than I could ever measure, and there have also been times that were so painful and disorienting and excruciating and agonizing that I wondered whether I was done.

**Finding your ikigai will be endlessly challenging.**

This is normal. Yes, it's frustrating when you hate your job, but finding your ikigai can also be maddening even if you know exactly why you're here and you get paid to do work that you love.

Twice I have experienced serious burnout.

And by burnout, I don't mean I was really tired and just needed to rest. Or I simply hadn't taken a vacation in a while and needed to get away.

By burnout, I mean curled up in the fetal position on the floor of my office, unable to move. The first was in February of 2004, and I was at my end. Drained in the center of my being. Nothing left to give. In the words of my therapist, whom Kristen drove me to see that night,

*You've been going too fast and too hard for too long.*

Which is why I told you about preaching that first sermon. I stumbled into work I love in my early twenties. And I could get paid to do it? Incredible! But no matter how simple and straightforward it may appear, your ikigai may at times leave you slumped on the floor.

**Embracing your ikigai will always require tremendous faith and courage.**

When you're starting out—or starting over—it can be hard to imagine that there's a life of satisfying contribution out there somewhere for you. The idea of having something to get you out of bed in the morning that you actually enjoy doing can seem like an illusion, a fairy tale for people who don't know how cold and lonely the world really is.

This is why it's absolutely vital for you to embrace at the outset the idea that you are a divine piece of work, created to do good in the world. The universe is not neutral or, worse, against you. When you set out to find your path, the universe is on your side. That is the faith that keeps you going.

We're all a work in progress, dealing with the voices filling our minds and hearts with destructive messages, searching for that sense of satisfying contribution, trying new things, all of it out of a desire to find what it is that will get us up in the morning.

**Your ikigai may involve a plan.**

I know a doctor who is deep in debt. He has other things he wants to do beyond being a doctor, but his school debt limits his options. We were talking one day about his restless sense that life was passing him by, and I asked him how soon he could erase that debt. He said he could do it in three years. I asked him whether he could do what he's currently doing for three years if he knew that that would be the end of this chapter of his life and the start of a new one. He got really excited about this plan. Your ikigai might involve an intentional step you're taking now to end this phase of your life so that you can start another one.

## Your ikigai may involve someone else for now.

I know a man who has several jobs doing menial work that he doesn't love. But he does love his son. And the money that he makes from those jobs he spends on creating a better future for his son.

Whenever I see this man, he's smiling. He talks about the honor of his work. He gives me updates on his son's schooling and work and life.

If a good portion of your energies are given to the well-being of another person, that's okay. It's not just okay, it's honorable. It's beautiful.

That's your ikigai for now. It may change over time. It probably will.

# The Bus Route

**One more truth about your ikigai: You may already have found it.**

Sometimes it's as straightforward as thinking differently about what you're already doing. Sometimes you discover your ikigai by understanding what you do in a whole new way.

My friend Liz told me a story about a bus driver in New York City. His route takes him all over Manhattan, and at his last stop everybody gets off before he drives the bus over the bridge into Long Island where the bus is parked overnight.

As he's pulling the bus up to the last stop, he tells the people on the bus to give him their problems. He tells them he knows that life is difficult and many of them are taking home from a day of work all kinds of burdens and anxiety and conflict—so why not leave all that with him so they don't take it home to the people they love the most?

He tells them that he'll take their burdens and drive them across the bridge so that they don't have to carry them around anymore.

It's a great story.
Strange and beautiful and moving.

I love this story because driving a bus can easily appear like a mundane job. Like he's *just* a bus driver. The power of the story is that he's more than *just* a bus driver. He's doing something far more significant than *just* getting people around town.

Sometimes we discover our ikigai by dropping the word *just* from whatever it is we do all day, refusing to say that we are just a _____ and instead opening ourselves up to the possibility that more is going on in whatever it is that we do all day.

Sometimes just that little shift in perspective can be all you need to get you out of bed in the morning.

# PART 4

# The Thing About Craft

*It's always weird when I see words like "old guard" and "veteran" next to my name. . . . I feel like I'm still figuring it out.*

—Carlton Cuse

I once had an idea for a tour.

I'd been reading a lot of quantum physics and then I came across a fascinating analysis of the Hebrew words in the first chapter of the Bible and somehow that connected with what I'd read in a book by a Scottish schoolmaster from the 1800s and that reminded me of something that had happened with my boys and me several years before—and gradually I began to see a talk forming.

And the more I worked on this talk, the longer it got. An hour, an hour and a half. It kept growing.

As I continued to work on this talk, I could see that most of it was based around sketches I was doing, simple drawings that could be done on a sheet of paper or a whiteboard.

I also had the strong sense that when it was ready, I should give this talk every night for a number of nights in a row, each night in a different city.

It was a *tour talk*.

I talked to my friend Zach who's in a band, and he agreed to introduce me to his booking agent. So Kristen and I drove to Chicago to try to persuade TimTheBookingAgent that he should book me into small clubs and theaters around the country. It makes me laugh now to think of a pastor pitching a rock promoter on doing a club tour to talk about quantum physics and Hebrew spirituality and charging money for the tickets. But he was up for it and booked a tour. (Twenty-five U.S. cities in twenty-eight days, for the record.)

I'll never forget the day we put the tickets on sale, wondering whether anybody would buy them. Eventually opening night came, we got on the bus, and away we went.

At first, it was all new, as it is when you're starting anything. Whether it's a tour or a charity or a child or a job or a team or a fund-raising effort, at first it's new. Whatever it is, it runs on new fuel.

**New fuel is a particular kind of fuel. Whatever you're doing is exciting, novel, fresh—the details sparkle and shine.**

But new fuel quickly burns out.

**Beware of new fuel.**

Any CEO or mom or dad or regional manager or middle-school teacher can tell you this—that first

day, first week, first month, first year is exciting and
daunting and you're filled with the adrenaline of a
new venture. And then something happens, something
unavoidable, something that it's absolutely crucial you
pay attention to . . .

You discover why you're doing this work.

Because whatever romance there is in writing or
speaking or touring or being an executive or running
an urban garden project or doing humanitarian work
or being a lawyer or nurse or teacher or manager
or architect or having your own store or starting a
charity—when the newness wears off, you are left
with the pure undiluted slog of the work.

**And you either love the work,
or you don't.**

It's one thing to do it because you want to be known
or liked or famous or respected or make lots of money.
And some people do their work for those reasons.

But those reasons get old and lose their power.

**You can run on that kind of fuel for only so long.**

And you very rarely see someone who's motivated by
those reasons thrive and endure and enjoy this work
over a long period of time.

# The Corvette

I loved giving that same tour talk night after night after night because I loved the craft of it. I loved telling those stories and trying to communicate the concepts in a certain way so that it created a particular kind of atmosphere in the room. I felt like I was working with clay, molding it and shaping it and forming it, night after night, learning new things about that talk and its contours and textures and the possibilities present in the content. It was deeply humbling, because no matter how well it went, I could always find ways to make it better.

I found myself nine nights in, seventeen nights in, twenty-three nights in—somewhere in the Deep South or on the East Coast or in the Pacific Northwest, in a club with no air-conditioning and low ceilings and bad lighting, about to go on, so incredibly happy. Like I was born for this. I'd be standing backstage, stomach full of butterflies, saying to whoever would listen, *How great is this? Can you believe it? I get to go do this again!*

I clearly remember thinking that if only eleven people showed up, I would still give it everything I had.

**There is a difference between craft and success.**

Craft is when you have a profound sense of gratitude that you even get to do this.

Craft is when you relish the details.

Craft is your awareness that all the hours you're putting in are adding up to something, that they're producing in you skill and character and substance.

Craft is when you meet up with someone else who's serious about her craft and you can talk for hours about the subtle nuances and acquired wisdom of the work.

Craft is when you realize that you're building muscles and habits that are helping you do better what you do.

Craft is when you have a deep respect for the form and shape and content of what you're doing.

Craft is when you see yourself part of a long line of people who have done this particular work.

Craft is when you're humbled because you know that no matter how many years you get to do this, there will always be room to learn and grow.

Success is different.

When I was in high school, we lived down the street from a family with three boys. The dad was a doctor, and I often stayed with their boys when Doc and his wife went out. They'd come home at the end of the evening and we would sit up and talk late into the night. One evening I went down to their house and there was a brand-new Corvette in the driveway. This was Okemos, Michigan, in the mid-eighties, and a Corvette was the ultimate sign that you'd made it. We stood in the driveway and stared at the car for a while. It was clear to me that Doc had arrived.

And then a few months later I went back to their house one evening to stay with their boys and there was a For Sale sign in the window of that Corvette. Huh? I asked Doc why he was selling his Corvette and he told me,

*All my life I've wanted a Corvette. And then I got enough money to buy one, so I did. And then the other day I walked out into the garage and thought, "I own a Corvette."*

That was his explanation—
*And I thought, "I own a Corvette."*

Do you know this feeling? You work and work and work for something and then you finally get it and there is a dull thud somewhere in your spirit? The kind of thud that comes from being let down. Like it didn't deliver. Like it isn't all it's cracked up to be.

*This was what I was working for all those years?*
*This?*

Goals and plans are fine, and they can often be effective motivators, but success promises something it can't deliver. As soon as you reach your goal, success creates a new one, which creates new anxieties and stresses.

Success is when you're seduced into thinking that your joy and satisfaction are not *here* but *there*—somewhere in the future, at some moment when you accomplish X or you win Y.

Success can never get enough.

It makes your head spin, because you get that thing you were desperately working for, for all those years, and when you get it, you realize that it isn't what you thought it was.

**Success says, *What more can I get?***
**Craft says, *Can you believe I get to do this?***

# Honor and Privilege

One Monday morning at sunrise I was walking down
the steps to the beach at one of my favorite surf
breaks. At the bottom of the steps were two city
workers in navy chinos and light blue shirts with their
names stitched above the pocket. One was probably
in his fifties, the other was in his twenties. They were
standing over a trash can, and the older one was
showing the younger one the proper way to change the
plastic bag.

Craft is noble.
Craft is old school.
Craft is one person showing another at 6:45 in the
morning the right way to collect trash.

Whenever you see someone taking his craft seriously,
it's inspiring, especially in work that often appears at
first glance to be menial and routine.

I see the same dignity and honor when I drop my daughter off at school in the morning and the principal of her school is standing out front, greeting the students as they arrive for another day.

*What would it look like for you to approach tomorrow with a sense of honor and privilege, believing that you have work to do in the world, that it matters, that it's needed, that you have a path and you're working your craft?*

# Reconnected

When you start out on your path, there's often a purity to the work, a romantic sort of idealism that drew you to it. Being an engineer, having kids, running a clinic, owning a bakery, practicing law—we have these images in our heads of what that looks like and it sounds slightly exotic and we're thrilled that we're finding our place in the world.

And then we get into it and we discover that some people can't be trusted and we spend a tremendous number of hours on distracting details and sometimes we pour our energies into a particular project or person and it falls apart and we're left wondering, *Why is this so difficult?*

Your business partner takes the money and leaves town, the kid you raised wants distance from you, the student you've been teaching decides to drop out, the people you've been leading criticize you.

**No one gets a free pass from heartbreak, discouragement, and the dull, weary thud that comes from asking,** *Did I waste my time?*

Over the years, that initial energy and enthusiasm can easily dissipate as life beats you up. You find yourself growing cynical.

You lose your passion.

This is why craft is so vital.

**You can find the craft in whatever you do.**

It's in there somewhere.
If you run a gas station or you do people's taxes or manage a call center, ask yourself what the craft is in that work.

Too many people have a job and they get a paycheck and that's it. Few things will inject more meaning and even, at times, joy into your work than seeing yourself working your craft.

*Whatever it is you do all day, do you see it as a craft?*

Seeing your work as a craft rescues you. Craft centers you. Craft reconnects you to your ikigai. The joy of waking up and having something to give yourself to . . .
that's what matters,
that's where the joy is,
that's where the life is.

# PART 5

# The First Number

*And that's when we began writing our own songs. . . . We knew we had something; you could feel it, the hairs stood up on your arms, it just felt so different. We didn't know what it was, but we liked it. I just came up with this riff for "Black Sabbath." I played "dom-dom-dommm." And it was like: that's it! We built the song from there. As soon as I played that first riff we went: "Oh God, that's really great. But what is it? I don't know!"*

**—Tony Iommi**

I once had an idea for a novel.

The idea came from a strange, surreal story someone had told me that was true. *And it involved me.* Somehow hearing that story sparked something in me and suddenly I had one scene and one line of dialogue.

That was it.

Once I realized I had that one scene with that one line, I realized I also had a character. And then another. And these characters had names, like Yves and Faruq. And then another character came out of nowhere who for some reason always wore sandals with odd-colored socks, and another character emerged who drove a gold Ford F–150 pickup truck with mud flaps.

Somewhere in there another character emerged named Rooster. He was the one who says the first line of the book, which I had as well.

So I wrote all of this down.

And then I thought of the ending. And then a twist that would come before the ending. Within a year I had pages and pages of scenes and dialogue and names of people and places. I knew that in that one particular conversation in that one scene toward the end that one character needed to be wearing a T-shirt that had this one particular phrase written on it.

This continued for years. Literally. Years.

I kept thinking to myself, *Is this a novel?*

Followed by, *How does a person write a novel?*

I did not know how to write a novel.

But I did know the first line.

So one day in the fall of 2008 I sat down at my laptop, stared at that blinking line, and then wrote the first line of that novel.

Far too often, we don't start because we can't get our minds around the entire thing. We don't take the first step because we can't figure out the seventeenth step.

But you don't have to know the seventeenth step. You only have to know the first step. Because the first number is always 1.

**Start with 1.**

# Step 1

That's where you start. With 1.

It's too overwhelming otherwise. It's too easy to be caught up in endless ruminations: *What if Step 4 doesn't work?* or *What if there isn't money for Step 11* or *What if people don't like the results of Step 6?*

You have no idea what the answers are to any of those questions. The only thing that wondering and speculating will do is separate you from the present moment.

When you begin, the seventeenth step is sixteen steps away.
You don't have to know how to do it,
or what it is,
or even *when* it is.

Because the first number is always 1.

It's not 5, then 8, then 24, then 62.7.

It's 1, then 2, then 3.

Your 1 may be making a phone call or an appointment or filling out a form—it may be a fairly simple task and yet it may seem like the biggest, most impossibly massive task in the world.

This is very normal, and it's only natural that it will feel at times like your shoes are made of cement and dialing that number takes more strength than lifting a house.

To do anything new—to do the 1—requires tremendous mental fortitude to not think about 2 or 3 yet.

That time will come. And it is not now.

Now is the time for 1.

You start with 1. And you work on that. Just 1. And when 1 is done, you move to 2.

You break it down into the next step and only the next step—
the next sentence
the next phone call
the next meeting
the next word.

Some people are stuck.

And they remain stuck.

And they don't get unstuck, because they can't get their minds around the whole thing.

But you don't have to get your mind around the whole thing, you only have to get your mind around the 1.

This is true when you're starting out, taking on new work, doing something you haven't done before; it's true at 2:37 on a Tuesday afternoon in October, and it's true for whatever it is you have in front of you during the next few hours.

What is your 1?

At any moment in the day, you can do only one thing at a time. And the more intentional you are about knowing what your 1 is, the more present you will be.

# Overthinking

I have a friend named Eddie. Over the past few years we've spent countless hours surfing together because we both love the same break near where we live. Eddie has long curly hair and usually surfs in a trucker hat so his hair sticks out the sides and he's always smiling.

I have a friend named Greg who surfs that same break Eddie and I surf. Greg works in finance. His area of expertise is in analyzing massive amounts of data in the global commodities market. That last sentence is about the extent of my comprehension of what he does. He is, obviously, very intelligent.

One day I paddled out and Eddie and Greg were already in the water because Greg had hired Eddie to coach him. Eddie is an excellent teacher, and when Greg took a wave in, I commented to Eddie on how good Greg is getting. Eddie said that Greg's only challenge was

to not overthink it. He then leaned in and smiled his
Eddie smile and said,

*I keep telling him, "Stop thinking about shit that ain't
happenin'."*

Is this you? You're here, in the middle of your day,
doing whatever it is you do, but your mind is all over
the place, thinking about 2s and 9s and 47s, playing out
possible scenarios, wondering about certain outcomes,
constructing conversations in your mind about what
you'll say and then what they'll say and then how
you'll respond—*thinking about shit that ain't happenin'.*

My friend Chico—that's not his real name, but if I'm
going to give him a fake name, it ought to be a good
one, right?—runs a large nonprofit organization.
He was telling me one day that he has all these big
questions about where they're headed and how their
work is going to evolve and how the challenges of the
city they work in are changing and what adjustments
all that is requiring his organization to make. He told
me that these questions are literally keeping him
awake at night. He said,

*There's so much to do! How do I know what to do next?*

But then, toward the end of our conversation,
he mentioned that there's a key person in the
organization who isn't on the same page as he is. He
said it's a growing problem because he has to keep

monitoring this person's work and correcting the work this person had done that isn't in line with where the organization is headed.

Do you see the problem? Chico has his 1. He's overwhelmed with all the work that needs to be done, but there's a 1 right in front of him. He has the wrong person in the wrong place. He needs to change that. He has a 1. And yet what keeps him awake at night are the 6s and 11s and 24s.

**Start with your 1.**

# Suspend Judgment

I once had an idea for a short film.

I'd been giving sermons for a while and people had been suggesting that we film them. But I'd seen that done before and I didn't find it very compelling. I had this sense that there was a way to film a sermon cinematically, with scenes and images that organically connected to the message. I'd been talking about this with some friends who agreed to form a creative company and figure it out. I then wrote a script based on a parable I'd told about something that happened to my one-year-old son and me. We went over that script draft after draft after draft until we were satisfied that it would work as a film.

And then we raised money. We were thinking maybe the film could play on television, which for a half-hour show meant the film would need to be twenty-two to twenty-three minutes long.

We filmed for almost a week, the footage was edited, and then the producer showed me a rough cut they'd made from the usable footage.

A rough cut that was ten minutes long.

This was a problem, because people had given money to see a twenty-two-minute film, not a ten-minute film.

I remember watching it and having two very strong reactions:
*What will we tell the people who gave us money?*
followed by
*I haven't seen anything like this before.*

We carried the rough cut around on a VHS tape (remember those?) and showed it to a number of people. No one mentioned the length. And everyone wanted their own copy.

**You start with your 1, and then you suspend judgment on what you're doing, because you don't know what you have when you start.**

No one does.

When you are constantly judging what you're doing, you aren't here. You aren't present. You are standing outside of your life, looking in, observing.

The time for judgment will come at some point, but in the moment, you have only the 1. And then the 2. And then the 3 . . .

In the case of those short films, we ended up making something shorter, *but, in the end, better* than what we set out to make.

The first number is always a 1.
You don't know what you have when you start,
and so you suspend judgment on whatever it is you're doing while you're doing it.

# Nerves

I once had an idea that involved lots of memorizing.

I was giving a series of sermons on the book of
Ecclesiastes and the more I studied the first three
chapters, the more I pictured the wisdom teacher
sitting in a palace at the end of his life, trying to
explain to someone younger what he'd learned from
his full and turbulent days. It became less and less
an ancient text to me and more and more a personal
confession, like I could feel the teacher's heart behind
the words.

As I worked through how to present my image of the
teacher, I had a growing sense that the best way to
explain how it must have felt to hear him wax on like
that would be to memorize the first part of the book
and then deliver it like a speech, a rant, a confession
while I walked through the audience. Which meant

I had to memorize it, and then beyond that, I had to know it, feel it, own it. (The actors reading this are thinking, *Yes, it's called acting.*) I remember standing in the back of the room about to start with butterflies in my stomach, realizing that I had absolutely no idea how it was going to go.

If you are working on something, about to deliver it, moments from opening the doors, an hour from everybody arriving, a week from the release date, two minutes from getting the results back, and you have butterflies in your stomach, be grateful.

You are in a wonderful place.

**Nerves are God's gift to you, reminding you that your life is not passing you by.**

**Make friends with the butterflies.**

Welcome them when they come,
revel in them,
*enjoy them,*
and if they go away,
do whatever it takes to put yourself in a position where they return.

**Better to have a stomach full of butterflies than to feel like your life is passing you by.**

# What You Don't Know

As I walked through the congregation, delivering those lines from the book of Ecclesiastes, I realized it wasn't what I was expecting—I thought it would feel big and profound, like an announcement about how the world works. Instead, it felt small and intimate, like I was confessing something. I wasn't expecting it to have such emotional resonance. Because usually when you're teaching about what someone else said, you talk about that person in the third person. But when you take a shot at *being that person,* it changes everything.

Now it's direct,
provocative,
unavoidable,
electric.

**We work hard to outline and plan and design and estimate and organize whatever it is we've set out to**

**do, all the while keeping in mind that when we start, we don't actually know what we have on our hands.**

It may be rubbish.
It may be brilliant.
It may be shorter or wider or longer or taller or louder or quieter or bigger or smaller than we originally thought.
We don't know, and so we suspend judgment. Right now, all we have is the satisfaction of doing it.

You don't know exactly what you have on your hands.

# The Ramp

When I was thirteen years old my favorite thing to do was ride my BMX bike. I rode trails, I learned tricks, but the thing I did most was go off jumps. I couldn't get enough of that feeling of flying through the air.

At the edge of our driveway was a stretch of grass that led to a swing set, about twenty feet from where the grass met the pavement. I decided that I would build a ramp so big I could leave the pavement, go off the ramp, and land next to the swing set.

So I set out to find the materials. We lived on a small farm at the time, and there were seven buildings on the property where my dad stored wood and paint and tools. I remember going through those buildings, searching for just the right pieces of wood, rummaging around looking for just the right nails.

When we're young and we want something, we do whatever it takes.

When you're in the store and you see something you want, you ask your dad over and over and over. You drive him crazy until he gets it for you or gives you one of those definitive no's that keep you quiet.

When it rains and you're stuck inside, you build a fort using every single blanket and cushion in the house.

When it's a summer night and you're outside with the kids from the neighborhood, you find a can or a flashlight and you invent a game.

You make things,
you find what you need,
you hunt down the supplies,
you do this instinctively.
You figure out what the 1 is and then you don't rest until you've got it.

Somewhere along the way in becoming adults, it's easy to lose this potent mix of exploration and determination. We settle. We decide this is as good as it gets. We comfort ourselves with, *It could be worse.*

If your life isn't what it could be,
if you know there's more,
if you know you could fly higher,
then it's time to start building a ramp.

I wanted that feeling of flying through the air,
but to get it I had to use nails and paint and wood.

That's how it works.
You want a better life?
You want to find your path?
You want an ikigai?

Find a 1.

## PART 6

# The Dickie Factor

*Your life has been a mad gamble. Make it more so. You have lost now a hundred times running. Roll the dice a hundred and one.*

—Rumi

I once told my boys some stories about Dickie Shoehorn. (Where did that name come from? I have no idea. But I love it. It still makes me laugh.)

I told them about the time Dickie went to his friend Joe's birthday party and gave him a helmet but it turns out Joe had a massive head so all the boys spent the rest of the time trying to fit that small helmet on that huge noggin, including dropping Joe off his roof headfirst while some of them held the helmet upside down on the ground.

I told them about the time Dickie was staying at his uncle Vince's house and was so excited about the cereal he was eating that he said he would swim in a pool of it if he could. Which is what Uncle Vince did, draining his swimming pool and then filling it with milk and cereal so Dickie could swim in it. Dickie learned that day that you actually *can* have too much of a good thing.

I told them stories about Dickie riding his bike and Dickie going to his favorite record store and making friends with squirrels—there was no end to Dickie's adventures.

At the end of a particularly good Dickie story we would shout, *DICKIE LIVES!*

After a year or so of making up Dickie stories, I thought, *I should write these stories down.*

So I typed one of them up and after working on it for a while, I showed it to my friend Alan who's a cartoonist. I told Alan all about Dickie and described some of the adventures Dickie had recently been on, and then I asked him if he'd draw me Dickie Shoehorn. And here's the amazing thing: Alan's drawing of Dickie looked exactly like Dickie.

I was so thrilled.

Alan then illustrated one of my Dickie stories. It came out better than I ever could have expected.

Then I tried to get the book published. I showed it to some publishers, telling them how this story was the first in a series called "The Adventures of Dickie Shoehorn." I talked about the potential for an ongoing cartoon show. I sent them the picture that would go on the home page of the website. I described the T-shirts we'd make with *Dickie Lives!* printed in big letters on the front. I had so many ideas. This was Dickie Shoehorn, after all, and what we've learned from Dickie is that life is an adventure and all sorts of things are possible . . .

But nobody was interested. Not one publisher. No one had even the slightest interest in seeing Dickie live.

And so I put the book in a file in a crate in my garage, and that's where it's been to this day.

**Whenever you create anything, you take a risk.** And that includes your life.

It may work out, it may not.
It may be well received, it may not be.

Sometimes you do things and you get results and that effort leads to more effort which leads to more results and away you go, success building on success. And then other times you try something new and it ends up in a crate in your garage because no one is interested.

**Whoever you are and whatever your ikigai is and however you move in the world, it always involves risk.**

Often when we face our blinking line the first thought that comes to mind is,

*This is risky.*

Which is true. It's always a risk to take action. It might not work, it might blow up in your face, you might lose money, you might fail. No one may get it.

But that's not the only risk.
**There's another risk: the risk of not trying it.**

How is *not trying* a risk? You risk settling and continuing in the same direction in the same way, wondering about other paths and possibilities, believing that this is as good as it gets while discontent gnaws away at your soul.

I remember asking a man with a Ph.D. who has had the same job for more than a decade what keeps him inspired in his work, and he sighed and said, *Well, not much—once or twice a year I hear something that's kind of encouraging* . . .

You could see in his eyes as he said this that he's bored, weary, cynical—somewhere along the way he settled, buying into the lie that *this must be as good as it gets.*

**There are always two risks. There's the risk of trying something new, and there's the risk of not trying it.**

You may write the book and no one is interested. You may decide not to write the book and then find yourself wondering, *What if I had made that book* . . . ?

**Either way there's risk.** And sometimes stepping out and trying something new is actually the less risky thing to do.

The question is,

*What are the two risks here?*

and then,

*Which path is actually less risky?*

# Deep Waters

There is a place within each of us that is the source of our life—it's the well, the tank, the engine, the overflow in our soul that we live from. In the wisdom of Proverbs it's the place in our being *where the waters run deep*.

Sometimes this place is overflowing with life, and sometimes it feels drained and empty. Certain actions and ways of life choke it and starve it and smother it; others cause it to hum with life and vitality.

My friend Chris had an idea for a new business. He and a friend resigned from their jobs, rented a small room with two desks, and then sat there every day starting that business from scratch.

He didn't know if it was going to work,
he had no guarantees,
he just sat there, day after day, working.

He didn't make any money that first year. He worked every day for a year and didn't make one dollar.

And yet he was more alive than ever.

It's possible to have emptied your savings account and be living in your friend's basement riding your bike everywhere because you can't afford a car and yet feel like you're bursting with vitality.

It's also possible to have lots of money in the bank, living in the house you had custom built, going on expensive vacations to exotic places, and yet you're miserable.

When you are bored,
restless,
longing for something more,
unfulfilled,
feeling like you've settled,
haunted by the sense of being trapped in your own life,
these are the deep waters of your soul speaking to you,
telling you something is wrong, something is missing,
something needs to change.

It's written in Proverbs that it *takes insight to draw out those deep waters in your heart.*

Sometimes we don't take the risk because of something that happened in the past. We tried something and it blew up in our face and so whenever there's a new opportunity all we can think about is what happened back then.

*Is this you? Are you dying where you are right now but unable to take a leap forward because it seems too risky?*

If you stay there, you may continue to feel like you're dying—

**now *that* is risky.**

# Failure

Risk sometimes leads to failure, **and failure is overrated.**

Your business went bankrupt, but when you talk about it years later you realize how much you learned from the experience, how much it humbled you, how much it realigned your priorities, how much it made you a better person.

It was *bad,* but it also produced an extraordinary amount of *good* in your life.

You went through a divorce and it left all sorts of scars, but you are a far more compassionate and courageous person because of that experience. Your marriage ended, and yet that ending started something new in your life. It was awful, but what has come out of it has been good.

Your friend died of cancer and to this day you miss her, and yet her death woke you up to the incredible gift that your life is . . . . It was so sad, and yet you now live with so much more gratitude.

You tried something new and made a complete mess of it, but now you don't live with that nagging question, *What if I had tried . . . ?*

*You now know.* You weren't successful at it, and yet it was something you needed to try.

You failed,
and yet that failure made you a better person.

You failed,
but it worked in your favor.

You failed,
but it made you stronger, more resilient, more appreciative.

You failed,
but it created all sorts of new life and growth and maturity in you.

You failed,
but you're now realizing that failure isn't all it's cracked up to be.

This is the beautiful, counterintuitive, strange, unexpected, reliable mystery built into the fabric of creation that is at work every time we fail.

You tried.
You leaped.
You took a chance.
You risked.

You paid attention to your deep waters, and you came to the conviction that trying this is where the life is, and so you did it.

**That is not failure. That is how you create a life.**

You try things and you make things with the awareness that you are always taking risks. Whether you are trying something new or doing the exact same thing, it's all risky.

**Failure is simply another opportunity to learn.**
Another opportunity to explore, to grow, to find out who you are.

You try this.

You try that.

Some things go great.

Others crash and burn.

When you do crash and burn, ask yourself lots of questions about whatever it is that happened:

What can you learn here?

How will you see things differently moving forward?

*Why did I do that?*
leads to,
*What have I learned?*
leads to,
*How will I do it differently in the future?*

What you would have called a failure becomes another opportunity for increased clarity about who you are and what you're doing here.

# Alive

**The truth is, you want risk.**

Not too much that it overwhelms you,
but some.

You want some risk in your life.

Risk is where the life is.

One morning I was at the gym near our house when I
overheard a man telling his friend that he was going
to be DJ'ing on the local radio station that night. He
was holding a barbell in each hand, working his biceps,
saying to his friend that he had some butterflies in
his stomach because he had never DJ'd live on the air
before and he was really excited about it.

How many people actually listen to a local radio
station?

*Who cares?*

He was alive.

A little nervous.

Not quite sure how it would go.

Chatting with his friend about his big opportunity.

We love to believe that we are sophisticated, refined people with good taste and a calm, reasoned view of the world. But we're also very simple: We want a little risk in our lives because it keeps things interesting. It wakes us up, it gives us a sense that we're alive and breathing and doing something with our lives.

So did I fail when I made that Dickie Shoehorn book?

Of course not.

Because—say it with me now—

*DICKIE LIVES!*

# PART 7

# The Two Things You Always Do

*I can't dance like Usher. I can't sing like Beyoncé. I can't write songs like Elton John. But we can do the best with what we've got. And so that's what we do. We just go for it.*

—Chris Martin

I once found myself lying facedown in a pile of dust and trash underneath a Christmas tree plugging in the lights.

I was twenty-five, a few months into my first official job as a pastor. I had assumed that in my new role I would primarily be doing, you know, pastor things. Spiritual, religious things. *Important things*. One day one of the leaders I reported to told me he needed my help on a project. I went upstairs to discover that they had put massive Christmas trees all across the stage and he needed me to crawl under each one and plug in the lights—while he sat out in the pews and gave me directions. What I discovered as I got under those trees is that no one had cleaned the back of the stage in a long, long time because you couldn't see it from the seats. And there I was, crawling on my chest through years of accumulated dust and grime, gradually breaking a sweat trying to find those outlets in the dark, thinking,

*I didn't sign up for this.*

**Everybody has a Christmas tree story.**

It's the humiliating thing that happened when you were just starting out, when you hadn't earned anything, when you were at the bottom, when you were the rookie and no one cared what you had to say.

When you're starting out, or when you're starting over, you do whatever work you can. You take whatever opportunities you are given. You do it with a smile. You give it everything you have. You take notes, you ask questions. And when you get the chance to interact with someone who is doing what you would love to do someday, you lean in and you listen intently.

If you are the assistant to the regional manager for distribution services, throw yourself into being the best possible assistant to the regional manager for distribution services you can be.

If you sell little plastic widgets, be kind and helpful to every single person who comes in to your little plastic widget store.

If you are asked to plug in the lights under the Christmas trees, get down and start crawling.

**The first thing you have to do is throw yourself into whatever it is you're doing.**

A young man once walked up to me after a talk I'd given and asked me how he could do what I do. I asked him what that was. He said,

*I want to talk to large crowds.*

How do you talk to large crowds?

You first talk to whoever will listen.

When I was starting out I said "yes" to every single opportunity that came my way. I spoke at state fairs and jails and home groups and chapel services and outdoor festivals and backyards. I paid for my own gas to get there. I was heckled, I was criticized, people came to hear me just to tell me afterward how terrible I was. I've tripped and fallen off stages, numerous sound systems have literally blown up while I was talking.

Once I spoke in Chicago and partway through the talk I realized I had run out of things to say. I started speaking slower, I repeated things I'd said earlier in the talk, I tried pausing, hoping something new would come to mind. It didn't. Eventually I stopped and walked off the stage, totally humiliated.

One time I was chopping up jalapeño peppers during a talk to make a point and I inadvertently wiped my eyes. They swelled and began to burn. I was temporarily blind. On a stage. In front of three thousand people.

I've spoken at events where I was in between a juggler and a plate spinner, I've gone on right after the heavy metal band, just before the Lamest Interpretive Dance

Group Ever, and once I was speaking to a group of high
school students in a basement and a dog walked in. In
the backdoor, though the audience, across the stage
I was standing on. And then it walked out the door.
And no one acknowledged the dog. Like it was totally
normal.

**Throwing yourself into it begins with being grateful
that you even have something to throw yourself into.**

# The Mail Room

**Sometimes we don't throw ourselves into it because we believe the small things are beneath us.** What we don't understand is that what appear to be the small things are actually the big things. They're where it starts, and throwing yourself into them inevitably creates new opportunities for you.

I often meet people who have a very high view of their talents and abilities, convinced that they are destined for something more important than whatever it is they are currently doing.

They usually say things like,
*I just know there's something more important out there for me*
or,
*I'm too big for the role I'm currently in*

or,
*I'm better than this.*

If you are destined for something more, that "more"
will only happen because you throw yourself into
whatever it is you're doing. This will always involve
humbling yourself and doing whatever is in front
of you, like crawling around on a dirty floor under
Christmas trees.

*How does the David and Goliath story start?*

It starts with David bringing bread and cheese to his
brothers at the battle. It's as basic and menial a job as
there is—the kind in those days that you would give to
the youngest son.

*You want to conquer giants?*

Bring the cheese first.

# Original

**Sometimes we hold back from throwing ourselves into it because we think that the only work worth doing is something completely original that's never been done before.**

I was doing a Q&A at an event in 2012 and a man raised his hand to ask a question, introducing himself by saying that he was just an insurance agent. As we've seen, that little word *just* is a problem.

Have you ever been in a car accident and had to call your insurance agent? When you're standing by the side of the road staring at the smoldering wreck of what was formerly your primary mode of transportation, you don't want *just* an insurance agent to answer the phone. You want someone to answer who has given himself to being the best insurance agent he can possibly be.

No one is just a mom, just a construction worker, just a salesperson, just a clerk—because **you doing your work in your place at this time is highly original and desperately needed.**

It may have been done or said by someone else. That's a distinct possibility. It may have been done or said before.

But it hasn't been done or said by *you*. It hasn't come through your unique flesh and blood, through your life, through your experience and insight and perspective.

One of the most inspiring organizations I've ever come across is called Kids Hope USA. They run mentoring programs in schools in which volunteers come in once a week to help kids with their schoolwork.

That's it. They help kids for an hour a week.

And what they've discovered over time is that literacy rates among these kids who read with someone for one hour once a week rise significantly over time. And those literacy rates are directly related to how many of them will, or won't, spend time in the county jail ten to fifteen years later.

By helping these kids learn, these volunteers are literally lowering crime rates.

People have been helping kids to read for a long time now. It is nothing new, it involves no new ground-breaking techniques or advanced technology or sophisticated data. And yet someone started that program. And countless people have been helped in the process.

**You don't have to reinvent the wheel because you don't have to *invent* anything.**

Sometimes it's as straightforward as identifying a need and then doing something about it in the most simple and efficient manner possible. That alone may be the most original thing imaginable.

# Rejection

**Sometimes we don't throw ourselves into it because we put ourselves out there in the past and discovered that snipers were crouching on every roof.** We were shot down. Criticized. It blew up in our face. No one liked what we did. We believe we failed.

The actor Mark Ruffalo went to six hundred auditions before he got his first break. Six hundred NOs before the first YES.

A number of publishers rejected J. K. Rowling's first novel. They were very clear that no one makes money writing books for kids. Her book was about a boy named Harry Potter.

Find me one person who's doing something interesting in the world who hasn't felt the hot sting of a NO. Or a door slammed in the face. Or boos. Or a rejection

letter. Or a tepid reception. Or bankruptcy. Or gotten
fired. Or been interrupted by a dog.

When we don't throw ourselves completely into it
and we hold back our best efforts because of what
happened in the past, we are letting the past decide
the future.

*Is there any way in which you are holding back because you
were burned before?*

*Is there any way in which you need to let the past be the past
so that the future can be something new?*

*Are there any critical voices that are running on repeat
in your head, holding you back from giving it everything
you've got?*

# Surrender

First, we throw ourselves into it.

And then, at the same time,
we surrender the outcomes.

**We surrender the outcomes because we cannot
control how people are going to respond to us and
our work in the world.**

They may love it,
or they may hate it,
or they may not react to it at all.

They may love us,
or they may hate us,
or they may not even notice us.

At one point Jesus says something that his followers
find hard to accept and a number of them leave him.

He turns to the ones remaining and asks, *You do not want to leave me too, do you?*

Another time the people listening to him ask, *Aren't we right in saying you're possessed by a demon?*

Later, when he's about to be arrested and crucified because his friend Judas betrayed him, he asks Judas, *Are you betraying me with a kiss?*

And then there's this one word at the end of one of the accounts of Jesus's life where we read that Jesus has been resurrected and he appears to his followers and some worshipped and some *doubted*.

People may walk away,

they may totally misunderstand us (*aren't we right in saying that you are possessed by a demon?*)

they may betray us ( . . . *with a kiss?*)

they may in the end stand at a distance and not know what to do with us.

**You cannot control how people are going to respond to you and your work in the world.**

Surrendering the outcomes does not mean that we don't care or we aren't emotionally involved or we are indifferent to the results. We want to connect with people and move them and inspire them—and we want more kids to learn to read.

Surrendering the outcomes is not surrendering goals or plans or dreams or numbers or results or ambition.

**Surrendering the outcomes is making peace with our lack of control over how people respond to us and our work.**

**Surrendering the outcomes is coming to terms with the freedom people have to react to us and our work however they want.**

**Surrendering the outcomes is embracing the fact that there are no guarantees when it comes to results.**

Have you ever heard someone on a stage or in the office or the classroom doing the work, but he's simultaneously searching for someone to tell him how good, accomplished, skillful, or excellent he is? It's as if he's searching for applause in order to keep going. You can sometimes see it in their eyes, this deeply unfulfilled sense that they are incomplete, that they need the strokes and affirmation of others to be content.

We surrender the outcomes so that the gift we give will be given freely.

**If you are looking for a particular response to bring you joy, that response may never come.**

**The joy comes from being fully present in this moment. The reward is in throwing yourself into it right here and now.**

There's a moment when Jesus starts telling his disciples that he's going to die. He's headed to Jerusalem to confront the corrupt systems of religious power that oppress the poor and rob people of their dignity. Jesus understands that throwing himself completely into his mission will have a cost, an unavoidable cost that he must pay, ultimately with his life. His disciples are crushed, and one of them,

Peter-the-caffeinated-disciple protests, *No never!*

Jesus turns to him and says, *Get behind me, Satan!*

Jesus speaks harshly to Peter not because he's upset by Peter's care and love for him but because of the impulse lurking behind Peter's words.

Jesus has said YES, and that comes with a cost, an outcome, which turns out to be his death.

**NO is not an option.**

The philosopher Martin Buber wrote that there are
YES and NO
positions to life.

*Is there any way in which you are saying NO, and it's cutting you off from the depths of your life, so it's time to say YES?*

*Are there any small things that you have been skipping over, skimping on, sliding across the surface of—so it's time to treat them like they're big things, throwing yourself into them?*

You throw yourself into it,
and you surrender the outcome,
all at the same time.

# This Is Where I Start

A few years ago I was renting a car in San Francisco and I noticed while I was waiting in line that the woman behind the counter was really good at what she was doing. She had this quiet confidence about her, like she was running the place just by the sheer force of her presence. Have you ever seen this— someone doing a job so well that it stands out? When I got to the front of the line, we started chatting and I learned that she lives across the bay and that she gets up and walks to the train station to catch a 5:15 train every morning, and then she gets off the train and walks the rest of the way to be at the office when it opens at 7 A.M. She works twelve hours and then walks back to the train station for the hour-long ride back across the bay and then she takes a bus or walks the rest of the way home.

*Three and a half hours of commute every day?*

Yes, she said, that's how long it takes.

She told me that this particular branch of the rental
car company is the busiest in the city and then she
smiled and said,

*This is where I start.*

That's a great line.

*This is where I start.*

You may be in the wrong place. You may feel
like you're not fully here because you need to be
somewhere else. Like another neighborhood. Or
another job. Or another city. Sometimes we feel like
we're standing at a distance from our own life because
we need to get another life. We need to leave one thing
and go to another in another place. That may be true.

But other times the reason we don't feel fully here
is rooted in how we're thinking about where we are.
After three minutes in that rental car office, I noticed
how fully present that woman behind the counter
was. It was that noticeable. And then I started talking
to her and she said,

*This is where I start.*

She's got things she wants to do, places she wants
to go. But for now, what she said gives us a world of
insight into her actions:

*This is where I start.*

If you feel stuck in your life, like it's passing you by,
like there's something way better for you somewhere
out there and you're missing it, try this—try throwing
yourself into the small things and repeating to
yourself:

*This is where I start.*

If your work feels beneath you, or monotonous and
meaningless, **try giving it everything you have like
it's the only thing you have.**

The joy is in the work.

The satisfaction is found in knowing that you're here,
you're alive, and you get to make something with your
life.

You're throwing yourself into it,
and you're surrendering the outcome,
at the same time.

# PART 8

# The Power of the Plates

*In the everyday world, you're just plugged into all the possibilities. Every time you get bored, you plug yourself in somewhere: you call somebody up, you pick up a magazine, a book, you go to a movie, anything. And all of that becomes your identity, the way in which you're alive. You identify yourself in terms of all that. Well, what was happening to me as I was on my way to Ibiza [for eight months of retreat] was that I was pulling all those plugs out, one at a time: books, language, social contacts. And what happens at a certain point as you get down to the last plugs, it's like the Zen thing of having no ego: it becomes scary, it's like maybe you're going to lose yourself. And boredom then becomes extremely painful. You really are bored and alone and vulnerable in the sense of having no outside supports in terms of your own being. But when you get them all pulled out, a little period goes by, and then it's absolutely serene, it's terrific. It just becomes really pleasant, because you're out, you're all the way out.*

—Robert Irwin

I've written this book sitting at my desk.

When I was first starting out I needed a desk but we didn't have any extra money. My friend Tomaas knew this and one day he picked me up and drove me to my favorite furniture store and bought me this desk. I've been sitting at it almost every day for more than fifteen years. In the mornings Kristen and I make our kids' breakfast and take them to school and then I sit down at this desk and I start in on the day's work.

On my desk is a lamp shaped like salad tongs. There's a pen some friends from South Africa gave me and a stack of thick white paper from a mill in Sweden. Next to the computer is an odd picture of two men walking that my sister gave me twenty years ago. There are some notes next to that picture for a talk I'm going to give. And that's about it.

I tell you about my desk and what's on it because when you're creating your life, finding your 1, throwing yourself into it, facing your blinking line,

**the details of your life are vital to your staying true to your path.**

Where you sit,
the tools you use,
the physical environment you inhabit,
the rhythm of your day and week,
the rituals that remind you who you are and what
you're doing here—
these details are important because

**how you do anything is how you do everything.**

No matter how distracted or weary I am, sitting down
at my desk centers me, reminding me that I have work
to do and that it matters.

Next to the heads (how can a sentence go wrong
when it starts with those four words? You remember
those heads—the ones the drummer from Puddle
Slug made?) a skateboard is hanging on the wall.
It's a Dennis Busenitz Pro model. When the REAL
skateboard company made this particular Dennis
Busenitz Pro model board, they misspelled his name
BUSENTIZ.

So what did Dennis do? He sold those boards for more
money as a limited edition TYPO board. How brilliant
is that?

Next to the board is a canvas print of a young woman
with a bandanna over her face and a can of spray paint
in her hand. She's just written on a brick wall,

*If you want to achieve greatness, stop asking for permission.*

Next to her is a guitar, a picture a high school girl gave me that she made out of torn-up pages from a Bible, a print of my wife Kristen, a surfboard fin, and a framed Larry Bird trading card.

I carried that Larry Bird trading card in my wallet everywhere I went for more than a decade until it started to wear out, and so I framed it and then got a new one for my wallet. My grandpa and I used to watch Larry Bird play basketball on Sunday afternoons. Grandpa would sit in his favorite chair and I would sit on the floor next to him and we would discuss how great Larry Bird was. Larry Bird wasn't the fastest and he wasn't the strongest and he couldn't jump the highest and he was pale and gangly, but he totally threw himself into the game. This meant something to me—a gangly kid with strange hair sitting there next to my grandpa in Williamston, Michigan, on those Sunday afternoons.

**The details matter.**

What you have hanging on the walls.
What's on your desk.
The stuff you fill your life with.

**There is a difference between *details* and *clutter*.**

Clutter is the books on your shelf that you're never going to read, the stacked-up papers that have been untouched for months, the endless flotsam and jetsam in your car, your closet, your garage, your kitchen, your bedroom, and your office.

Clutter is all those clothes that you haven't worn in years filling all those shelves and drawers.

Clutter is all those possessions you've got piled in the garage *just in case* you might need them someday. Even though it's been seven years since you first made those piles and haven't looked in them since.

Details are those pictures that remind you why you do what you do.

Details are those books that are filled with underlining and notes. Or the books that you actually will read.

Details are those few items of clothing that you actually do wear.

Details are those objects you use regularly that help you do better whatever it is you do.

Details are the tools of your craft.

Details remind you who you are, where you've been, and what your path is.

Our lawyer Nicole uses one kind of binder. When we meet with her, whatever it is we're talking about and whatever papers we have to sign are always in these particular binders. On the front of the binder is the logo of her firm, a small additional cost that you could easily argue doesn't make a bit of difference.

Except that it does.

It's a small detail, but I always notice it.

There is an elegance to the work that Nicole does, a dignity that she brings to her work that is inspiring. I see it in the wristband filled with pins that the tailor wears, in the worn leather tool belt around the waist of the construction worker remodeling a house down the street, in the pencil my friend Dave uses when he designs surfboards.

I point out these details because we are tactile creatures. Fabric, leather, graphics, paint, paper—these substances and surfaces we surround ourselves with powerfully affect us.

**Our external environments mirror our internal lives.**

If your desk is cluttered,
don't be surprised if you find it hard to focus.

If your closet and garage are piled with stuff you don't use,
don't be shocked when you are easily distracted.

If things are lying around your living and working space that don't serve a clear purpose, don't be amazed that you aren't very calm and centered.

If you often feel like you're in one place but your thoughts are ping-ponging from one idea to the next, examine the space you're in.

Is it clean?

Is it organized?

Does everything in it need to be there?

What would happen if you emptied that room and over the next few months brought in only the things that you need? How much of what is in there now would you bring back in?

How much of that stuff that surrounds you every single day is actually vital to your path, and how much of it is in the way?

We are integrated beings, everything in our lives connecting with everything else. When we feel like life is passing us by, like we're skimming the surface of our own existence, often the best place to start is with our material possessions. Clean out the closets and and bookshelves and garage, sort out what goes and what stays. Be ruthless. If you don't use it, toss it.

It's extraordinary how even small changes in your exterior environment can deeply shape your interior life. Clean, intentional physical space can dramatically affect how calm your mind and heart are.

# Rhythm and Sabbath

And so I sit here at this desk I've been sitting at for fifteen years and I do this work. I write this book. Work on a talk. Record a podcast. There's a window in the first part of the day when I create things, and then it closes. By lunch I'm no good on that front. No new ideas; it's like pushing a rock up a hill.

So I don't force it. I do other things. Going to meetings, answering emails, making phone calls, organizing trips—whatever else. And then by dinner I'm done. No more work for the day. We eat dinner, we watch sports, we go see friends, we walk the dog, we get groceries, we help the kids with homework, we play with Legos.

**There's a rhythm to the day because there's a rhythm to everything.**

You just took a breath. You're about to take another. Inhale, then exhale, then another inhale. In and out. There's a rhythm to your breathing. It's the same with nature. There's the gradual dying of fall, the death of winter, the spring with new life bursting everywhere you look, and then summer in all its fullness. And then fall comes again, and the rhythm continues.

There's the rhythm to waking and sleeping. When you wake up, your body is firing cortisol, which gradually tapers off as the day goes on. Cortisol is related to adrenaline, giving you the energy you need to go about your day. And then later in the day as the sun goes down your body ideally begins releasing melatonin, anticipating the end of the day when you will drift off into a deep sleep.

Have you ever checked your email just before going to bed and then found yourself wide awake staring at the ceiling at 2 A.M.? Of course. At just the moment when your body was most relaxed, ready to get the sleep it needs, you jolted it back to life with the light of the computer screen and new ideas and problems to solve and more things to do. Checking that email was out of sync with the natural rhythms of the day.

Breathing, nature, sleep—there's a rhythm to all of it.

And then there's my Friday afternoon ritual. Sometime around 4 P.M. I turn my computer off. When I do this, I always have the same physiological reaction: It's like my entire being takes a deep breath. I relax somewhere in my cells. I feel the release in my bones. I sigh like a great weight has been taken off my shoulders.

I turn my computer off knowing that I won't turn it back on until Sunday at the earliest. No email, no work, no creating, no writing. The workweek is done.

I started this ritual because my days used to look all the same. Monday looked like Sunday which looked like Saturday which looked like Thursday. Around that time someone told me that animals in a zoo demonstrate adverse behavior when they're left on display for more than six days in a row.

*What?* I'd never heard that. *There's a six-day rhythm built into creation?*

I was reading a book at that time about the Exodus story in the Bible and how the Hebrew slaves in Egypt had to make bricks every day.

Bricks, bricks, bricks—day after day. Every day the same. *That's* despair: when every day looks like every other day. But then these Hebrews are rescued from Egypt and brought out into the desert, where God commands them to set aside one day a week and do no work.

And some of them can't do it. They literally can't take a day off from work.

In Egypt, their worth and value as slaves came from how many bricks they produced. When they left that life, they left that understanding of what it meant to be a human being. And so one of the first things they are told to do is spend one day a week remembering that they are not slaves and that their worth and value do not come from how many bricks they produce.

One day a week to remind themselves that they are human beings, not human doings.

**What struck me about the story is that even though they get out of Egypt, it takes a while to get the Egypt out of them.**

Have you ever felt like you're just going through the motions?

Like you can't distinguish one day from the next?

Like you're a number, a cog in a wheel, a slave to a machine?

Like your worth and self-esteem are way too caught up in how many bricks you're producing?

Like how you think about yourself is inseparable from what you do?

Like you're a slave to your cell phone, your to-do list, your job?

This story about Egypt is a story about us. I was deeply convinced that I had some Egypt in me, that I was a slave to my work, and I needed help.

So Kristen and I decided to start setting aside one day a week that would be different from the others. In the Jewish tradition, this one day that is not like the others is called the Sabbath. I worked on Sundays at that time, so we decided that Saturday would be our Sabbath.

We asked ourselves: *What would make this day different from the other six? What would make it unique?*

For Kristen, most days she has a list of things she has to get done. For her, then, Sabbath would be the day without a to-do list.

For me, my work is creating things. So for my Sabbath, I wouldn't make anything.

We decided that we would let the day be whatever it wanted to be. We'd go see friends or take the kids somewhere or relax around the house. We asked each other,

*What feeds your soul?*

And then we did that.

Which sounds great—but it was not great. In fact, it made us miserable. Literally, by early afternoon on those first Saturdays, we were depressed. Sluggish.

Sad. Listening to Depeche Mode, wondering what the point of it all is.

What? This was supposed to be great! We had assumed that this day would be thrilling, like we'd tapped into the mother lode of energy. But it wasn't. It's been said that *the Sabbath gives the universe the energy it needs to continue for another six days.*

Where's that energy?
Where's that life?
What's wrong with us?
What's wrong with this day?

We couldn't figure it out. Why is this day so difficult? Why are we barely able to stay awake by the end of lunch? Why is it so hard just *being*?

Gradually, over those first few months of trying to treat one day differently from the rest, we began to understand what was happening. Most of our days we wake up and we *go*. School, work, store, lists, projects, loose ends—we call people and attend meetings and answer phone calls. Sound familiar?

All this motion is an endless stimulus for our bodies. Like a hit, or a drug. You see that you've just gotten a text and it sends a little ripple of excitement through you.

It's exciting to keep moving. If people are contacting you it means they're thinking about you, you're needed, you have a role to play, you matter—all of that affects us spiritually. It may be good, but it's also very seductive because it's easy to become addicted to the pace, to the hit.

It feels good to be needed by people.

*Have you ever checked your phone and found no new calls or texts or emails and you felt a bit let down?*

What Kristen and I discovered when we took a day and removed all of that constant stimulus is that our bodies fell into a state of shock, like our bodies were asking us,

*What are you doing to me?*

*Where's the hit, the excitement, the adrenaline spike?*

*What are we supposed to do—nothing?*

And so we crashed. Sitting there on the couch at 2:19 on a Saturday afternoon, listless, wondering what's wrong with us. The lack of speed and stimulus on this one day exposed the overload of stimulus and the insane pace of the other six days.

**When we spent a day being fully present, we quickly discovered how much of the rest of our lives we weren't fully present.**

For many of us in the modern world, our understanding of time is based on what we can get out of it. Time has a utilitarian function in our lives. We

work X number of hours in order to get Y amount of
money. We have twenty minutes left to get those three
things done.

We relate to time on the basis of what we can produce
within a certain amount of time.

How long it will take to do that.

How many hours of sleep we will get.

But when you begin practicing Sabbath, a day during
which you don't have a set schedule and you don't
have to be anywhere, you find yourself relating to time
in a different way.

Think about some of the most favorite moments
in your life. At those times, you might have said, *I
lost track of time.* Or you looked at your watch and
wondered, *Where did those hours go?* Or you remarked,
*That day just flew by.*

In those moments time fades because you are nowhere
else but in the present. Time isn't being used to
produce anything, it isn't being measured for what you
can get out of it. Spending one day a week relating to
time in a different way gradually influences how you
think about and relate to time during the other days of
the week.

**Sabbath leaks.**

It spills over.

It changes how you live the other six days.

**When you intentionally slow down,
you instantly see how fast you've been moving the
rest of the time.**

**When you stop to pay attention,
you learn how much you've been missing.**

Sabbath is a day when you act like the work is done,
even if it isn't.

Sabbath is when you spend a day remembering that
efficiency and production are not God's highest goals
for your life. Joy is.

Often on Sabbath I'd become aware that I was still
carrying around wounds and bruises I had sustained
during the week. But I had kept moving, on to the next
thing, and hadn't slowed down enough to feel them.

Have you ever had an ugly confrontation or
conversation with someone but when it was over you
had to go to the next meeting or event or place and so
you didn't have time to process it? And then days later
out of nowhere you realize that there's all this tension
and pain sitting just below the surface of your life, but
you've been moving too fast to deal with it?

Have you ever gotten really angry about something
trivial like a drawer in the kitchen not working right or

something falling off the shelf in the garage and you find yourself wondering, *Where did all that anger come from?*

It built up from days and days of moving too quickly, absorbing all the pain and anguish the world throws at us that we don't have time in the moment to think about and work through. It accumulates in our hearts, our cells, our psyches, expressing itself at the strangest times.

You're not that angry about the drawer in the kitchen. The drawer simply gave you an outlet for all the grief and pain sitting right below the surface of your life.

**Sabbath forces you to listen to your life.**

**Sabbath is a day when you are fully present to your pain, your stress, your worry, your fear.**

**Sabbath is when you let whatever you've pushed down rise to the surface.**

**Sabbath is a day when things that are broken get fixed, when things within you that have torn are mended.**

# Your Groove

What most surprised me when we started practicing Sabbath is how much it affected the other six days. The growing sanity of this one day exposed the insanity of the others.

**When you begin to practice a rhythm to your week, you begin to see the need for rhythm all the time.**

For example, lunch.

You sit down to eat with a friend and she puts her phone on the table between the two of you with the screen facing up. Without saying anything verbally, she has just communicated to you that even though she is here, with you at the lunch, about to order food, if that phone rings and that screen lights up, she will be with you, but not be with you. Here but not here. In that moment as she glances down at the screen she

will be making a decision about whether to answer
or not.

This extraordinary technology that makes it possible
for us to connect with someone on the other side of
the world also disconnects us from the person on the
other side of the table.

**To live with rhythm requires that you be intentional
about what you're doing and when you're doing it.**

If you're with a person,
then be with him, be with her.

If you're making phone calls,
then make phone calls.

If you're playing with your kids,
then play with your kids.

If you're having lunch and talking,
then be there. Put your cell phone away.

I'm going to type a word in the next line and when
you read it, notice the first feeling or associations that
come to mind. Ready?

*Inbox.*

Were you instantly at ease, relaxed, struck with how
much that word calmed you? Probably not. If you're
like me, your first association with that word is a

number—the number of emails that have come in since you last checked your inbox.

Emails are piling up while you read or listen to this book. Emails you will respond to . . . later. Do you see what just happened? In the course of a few sentences, you went from interacting with this book to also thinking about your emails, which you will deal with in the future.

People didn't used to have email inboxes. We have literally invented new ways to be stressed.

When do you deal with your email?

All the time?
Three times a day?
Constantly?

Is how you spend your day determined by who sends you emails and when they send them?

Or do you have set times when you deal with your email?

When is your cell phone on?
When is it off?
When can't we get ahold of you?
When don't you answer your phone because you're doing something?

Can we call you and interrupt what you're doing anytime of the day?

When are you working and when are you not working?

**Central to creating a life worth living is understanding that you have more power over your time than you realize.**

Inhale, exhale.
On, off.
Work, play.
Stepping in, stepping back.

**You create the rhythm that helps you do the work that you're here to do.**

Everyone I know who's been on their path for a while and thriving more than ever has details and routines they take seriously. Some people begin each day with a walk, others sit in silence for a set period of time every afternoon, some eat at the same restaurant every weekday for lunch, others wear an outfit or uniform when they work, some say prayers at certain times, some go for a run in the late afternoon.

How you order your time, how you arrange the physical space you work in, what you wear, the tools you use, the food you eat and the times you eat it, the people you meet with at set times—all these details matter.

Think about your rituals and routines like a muscle that you are building, each repetition making that muscle stronger and more resilient.

As you find your groove, knowing what part of the day this is and what you do and don't do in this part of the day, you will find yourself getting better at dealing with the unexpected debris that inevitably comes flying your direction.

# We Have This Morning

When Kristen and I were engaged, we registered for wedding gifts. And I learned in the process that you're supposed to have two kinds of plates.

Everyday plates. And then plates that you use only once in a while, for special occasions. These plates are called Fine China.

I also learned that when you register for things, you actually get a lot of those things. We received those two kinds of plates. The plates we use every day, and this second set of plates that we use only now and again. Those plates, the ones we seldom use, are for big occasions, big celebrations.

We used them once or twice a year.

And then we started practicing Sabbath. And I started to be more present, less distracted, less and less *there* and more and more *here*. And the more *here* I was, the more I learned that all we have is the present. All we have is today.

This is obvious, true, and revolutionary if you take it seriously.

So if you come over to my house tomorrow morning, and I'm making breakfast, you'll notice that we go all-out for breakfast.

Eggs, bacon (bacon: not that good for the body, but really good for the soul), sometimes French toast or pancakes, fresh smoothies—
we do it right.

And then you'll notice that we eat breakfast on the Fine China.

Because this day is all we have.
We are celebrating.
This morning.
We have this morning.
That's it.

There is power in the details,
power in this moment,
power in treating this meal as the sacred gift that it is.

Find your rituals,
develop your routines,
create those practices that ground and center you.

Stick to them,
don't apologize for them,
treat them, even the small things, like they're big
things.

Because they are.
They're huge.

There's power there.
Power in the details,
power in the ritual,
power in the routines,
power in those plates.

# PART 9

# The Exploding Burrito

*The meaning of awe is to realize that life takes place under wide horizons, horizons that range beyond the span of an individual life or even the life of a nation, a generation, or an era. Awe enables us to perceive in the world intimations of the divine, to sense in small things the beginning of infinite significance, to sense the ultimate in the common and the simple; to feel in the rush of the passing the stillness of the eternal.*

—Abraham Joshua Heschel

In the summer of 2000 I hit my head.

Actually, I hit my head several times. I was waterskiing, trying to learn a wakeboard trick called a Tantrum (just the name tells you there's going to be trouble . . .). It's a trick in which you jump the boat's wake and—still holding on to the rope—do a backflip, landing on the other side of the wake.

I was very focused on landing that trick that summer, and on this one particular Thursday in August I attempted ten or fifteen in a row. I wasn't getting it, and I repeatedly fell, the back of my head smacking the water each time.

Eventually I got in the boat to take a break, and that's when things got weird. Apparently, I wasn't making any sense, because my friend Kent asked me what day of the week it was. The last thing I remember is looking at him and saying, *I have no idea what day it is* . . .

Later I was told that Kent and MikeTheBoatDriver took me back to the dock, led me to the passenger seat of my car, and then drove me to the hospital. Kristen met us there, where we learned that I had a closed head injury, also known as a concussion. (Who gets a concussion from hitting their head on *water*?) I should say *they* learned, because I was out of it. I don't remember going back to the dock or driving to the hospital or talking to the doctor or any of it.

The first thing I do remember is being driven home, turning the corner onto our street and somehow going from being *out of* it to being *in it*—*in it* like never before.

Here's what I mean by being *in it like never before*: Let's say you're talking with your neighbor and as you're chatting about last week's heat wave you hear a dog bark a few houses over and you wonder whether that's the same dog you pass by on your morning run and just then your phone rings in your pocket while you notice a scratch on the bumper of your car that you hadn't noticed until now while you're responding to whatever your neighbor just said about the dust that's been building up on her windows while you note that the temperature is dropping because the sun is about to set and you remember that you still need to wash the carrots that you put in the sink before you went outside to get the mail and saw your neighbor . . .

Dogs,
bumpers,
windows,
carrots.

Sound familiar? You're standing there, physically present with your neighbor, but your mind is ping-ponging from one thought to another, noticing sounds and colors, processing random events from earlier in the day, connecting whatever your neighbor just said about the dust on her windows to the dust on your windows which reminds you that you need to take out the recycling when that thought is interrupted by remembering how you still haven't responded to that text about plans for Friday night—

**You're there, but you're also *not there*.**

You're in that place, at that time, standing there in the street, and yet—in a way that is hard to describe but very real—somewhere in your being you're also *not there*.

But in that moment coming home from the hospital when we turned the corner onto our street, I was there, in the front seat of the car, and nowhere else. Whatever it was that the concussion did to my brain, I wasn't able to think about anything that wasn't directly in front of me. The color of our house, the grass in the yard, the furniture as I walked in the back door—I noticed all of it, like everything was in slow motion and every detail was on fire.

It was familiar—I knew at some level that I'd been in this place before—but it was also unfamiliar, like I was seeing it all for the first time.

Imagine getting a tour of your life, as if you were observing your life from outside of your life. It had all the comfort and security of something I knew, but the electricity and thrill of something I hadn't encountered before.

And then our boys came into the room. I looked at Kristen and said, *These are our kids?* She told me their names as I stared at them. They were the most captivating, exotic creatures in the universe to me. I couldn't stop tearing up. I kept looking around, repeating, *This is our life?*

I asked Kristen about my job and where we went to school and how long we'd been married as if I didn't know the answers, even though the answers she gave resonated with what I already knew at some sort of cellular level, as if they were stored not in my mind but somewhere else in my being. She told me how we met and where we had lived in Los Angeles and I listened like it was the most interesting story I'd ever heard. Because it was.

I was on the edge of my seat hearing about my life, the life I had been living in the first place.

My friend Tomaas told me years later that he stopped by on that first day I was home and when he walked in the front door I was sitting in a chair, staring at my hand. He said that I watched it for a while and then turned to him and said, *Isn't it amazing?*

You know how shafts of sunlight stream through
the window and you can see specks of dust floating
in the air? (And your first thought is *I should vacuum
more*.) I would focus on a single speck and follow it
as it drifted leisurely down toward the floor, as if
it were the only thing on my mind. Because it was.
Literally. Ten or twenty minutes at a time with no
other thought running through my mind but that one.
particle. of. dust.

Kristen made me a burrito and when I took the
first bite, I had to put my fork down because of how
startling it was. I could taste all of the spices one at a
time, and yet also at the same time. Each one, and the
whole, together, simultaneously and separately.

Now I know what you're thinking at this point—you're
thinking, *Yes, Rob, this is why some people do drugs*.

True. But there's more to it.

My brain was busy remembering, reorienting itself
and plugging back in all those wires that got yanked
out when I hit my head. (I'm sure there's a neurologist
somewhere who just read that last sentence and shook
her head and thought, *It's way more complicated than
that . . .*). And because my mind was so occupied on
the task at hand, it didn't have energy for the many
other tasks that it normally performs.

Like thinking about the past. Regret, anxiety, ruminating on things I wished I'd done differently—I didn't have any of that because all that was *back there*, in the past, and I was only capable of being *right here*, in the present.

Or thinking about the future. All that worry and stress that we carry around, thinking about what might happen and how things might unfold and what might go wrong was *up there, ahead* in time. That was simply absent from my mind.

I could only be present. And the present was enough. It wasn't just enough, it was more than enough. It was overwhelming. The burrito wasn't just food, it was an explosion of sensation. The boys weren't just our kids, they were luminous and ineffably wondrous miracles of flesh and bone. Everything wasn't just our house and family and friends and life, it was a massive, majestic, complex, electrified gift that floored me with its radiance and vitality, filling me with overflowing gratitude. It was profoundly satisfying and more than I could bear, all of it charged and energized in all its Technicolor splendor.

I'm grasping at language here, trying to describe how transcendent and awe-inspiring it was to see things as they are in their fullness without distractions or guilt or chattering inner dialogue or comparing myself to others or wondering whether there's a better life somewhere else or wandering thoughts or any urgency to get to the next thing on the list or the next event on the calendar or the next email that needs a response.

There was no rushing, no racing, no frantic dash to grab car keys or get somewhere on time. Time itself warped and slowed around me, creating a serene stillness.

All I had was *now*, and *now* was enough. It wasn't just enough, it was more than enough.

# Presence

My life at the time was packed. Busy. Stressed. I was racing from one thing to another. We had a young family, the lawn needed to be mowed and the bills paid and diapers changed. We had just started a church. I was giving sermons and going to meetings and visiting people in hospitals and doing funerals and hiring staff and writing letters and discussing budgets. Around that time I did three weddings on one Saturday. That kind of packed. Every moment was scheduled. I would drive home from work and make calls that I hadn't had time to make during the day at the office and I'd still be talking when I got home so I'd sit in the garage still in the car trying to finish the conversation while my two-year-old son stood in the doorway wondering why I wasn't coming inside.

And then I hit my head.

And I couldn't work or accomplish anything. I'd sit there day after day, staring at my hand or a speck of dust, raving to whoever would listen about how magical and electric and sacred and amazing it all is.

If you had stopped by the house during that week I was recovering, you would have heard me ramble for five minutes and thought, *He is so out of it*.

But I was also so *in it*—in the moment, in the present, in my life—more than I'd ever been before.

I hadn't just tasted a burrito more fully, I had tasted life more fully.

And it changed me. Over the next week my memory gradually came back as the effects of the concussion wore off, but something had shifted within me.

I learned that my life—
my average, ordinary, routine, everyday life—
has infinite depth and dimension and meaning and significance.

I learned that the present moment, with all its pressure and heartbreak and work and struggle and tension and questions and concerns, is way more interesting and compelling and mysterious and even enjoyable than I had ever imagined.

You and I were raised in a modern world that taught us how to work hard and be productive and show up on time and give it our best. We learned at an early age that our grades in high school mattered because that was what colleges look at, and our work in college mattered because that's how we were going to get good jobs, and how hard we worked at those first jobs determined how fast we would climb the ladder and get ahead in our careers.

And so, for many of us, that's what we did. We put in the hours and saved our money and stayed late at the office because that's what one did to be successful.

But all that left us missing something. We were stressed. Distracted. Busy. Feeling like life was passing us by. We had a full schedule, but not a full heart.

We learned lots of very valuable skills, but we weren't taught how to be here, how to be fully present in this moment, how to not be distracted or stressed or worried or anxious, but just be *here,* and nowhere else—wide awake to the infinite depth and dimension of this exact moment.

That's what happened to me when I hit my head—I experienced something else, something so good and true and rewarding and satisfying, but I didn't know how to stay there. I realized that there were skills and knowledge and practices and muscles that I simply didn't have.

And so I set out to learn how to be here. I wanted to be present all the time, even when I was working and making plans and facing challenges and moving forward. I wanted to be *here* even when I went *there*.

There's a fascinating commentary in the ancient tradition about the story of Moses and the burning bush. The rabbis say that the bush didn't suddenly start burning when Moses came upon it; it had been burning the whole time. Moses was simply moving slowly enough and paying attention enough to actually notice it.

Are you moving so fast, are you so stressed and distracted, your head down reading your latest text messages and emails, that you're passing burning bushes all day long?

Whatever it is that you find yourself in the midst of on any given day—from laundry and meetings and traffic to going to class and answering emails and driving kids around—I want you to learn to live like you're not missing a thing, like your eyes are wide open, fully awake to the miraculous nature of your own existence.

# Seeing the Ocean

While I was writing this book I had lunch with my friend Cory, who, as soon as we sat down, told me a story. He reminded me that two years earlier he and I had been driving along the coast in my car and I kept pointing to the sea and laughing and saying, *That's the Pacific Ocean! Can you see it? That's the Pacific Ocean! Can you see it?*

I thought this was funny because when most of what you can see is the ocean, pointing it out is, well, funny.

He told me that at the time he was busy, stressed, working all the time, lying in bed at night obsessing about his job, and that when I pointed to the ocean and laughed and asked whether he could see it, he couldn't see it.

He then leaned across the table and said,

*Rob, do you get it? I was so lost in my head and distracted and stressed that I couldn't see it!*

Cory then told me that the experience deeply upset him because he felt like there was something he was supposed to see but he didn't. So he started making changes in his life, slowing down, obsessing less, enjoying more. And then he told me:

*I came here today to tell you that I can see the ocean now.*

Picture your life.

Let's start with the people you're closest to—
family
friends
spouse
partner
lover
kids
stepkids
siblings . . .

Now let's broaden the circle to include
neighbors
co-workers
acquaintances.

Now let's include the physical settings you inhabit,
from where you live
to where you play,
where you work,

where you go to get away from it all,
where you went for the best vacation ever,
where you exercise,
walk,
explore,
eat.

Now picture that person you love.

That's _____.

Do you **see** her?

Do you **see** him?

Do you see the ocean right in front of you?

Stand back and see that person you love from a slight distance.

Like you never have before.

Like you're meeting him for the first time.

Like you're getting a tour of your life and this is your first encounter with her.

Like I just pointed him out and said to you,
*This is* _____.

You begin asking me questions about her. You want details, dates. I tell you how you met him. I show you some pictures. It's coming back to you. This is new but it's familiar.

Now think of some of the other people you love. Picture people you work with. Imagine your neighbors.

What if you just learned that one of them has a life-threatening illness? What if you just learned you have a life-threatening illness and your neighbor came over to tell you how much you mean to her? What if your neighbor got done telling you that and then you told him how much he means to you?

What if you had no list of things to do, you had no regret and no worry and all you had is this moment and this second and this tour of your life?

**No one has ever done this before.**

**No one has ever been you before.**

This exact interrelated web of people and events and places and memories and desire and love that is your life hasn't ever existed in the history of the universe.

Welcome to a truly unique phenomenon.

Welcome to the most thrilling thing you will ever do.

Welcome to your life.

Welcome to here.

I want you to be here. I want you to see and feel and notice and even enjoy your life, not just as you sit quietly, but as you go, as you work, as you answer email, as you are stuck in traffic, as you find your path and throw yourself into it, surrendering the outcomes as you risk and learn and grow and work your craft, in the push and pull and stress and pain and sorrow and responsibility and slog of this sacred gift that is your life.

And if that could happen without you having to hit your head, how great would that be?

# Endnotes, Riffs, References, and Further Reading

**Part 1. The Blinking Line**

Alan Watts quote is from the *Tao of Philosophy*.

**. . . if I was going to write a book, I was going to have to actually write a book.** That book is called *Velvet Elvis*.

**Christopher Moore's book.** It's called *Lamb: The Gospel According to Biff, Christ's Childhood Pal*, and it's brilliant.

**Annie Dillard.** The line is from *Teaching a Stone to Talk: Expeditions and Encounters*: "What is the difference between a cathedral and a physics lab? Are not they both saying: Hello?"

**Dorothy Sayers's words about Trinitarian creativity** are found in her book *The Mind of the Maker*.

**Dave Eggers.** Please tell me you've read something by Dave Eggers. I'd start with *What Is the What*. Or maybe *The Circle*. Or probably you should begin with his first book, *A Heartbreaking Work of Staggering Genius*.

**This poem, by the way, is the first chapter of the Bible.** For a fascinating perspective on Genesis 1, see Charles Foster's book *The Selfless Gene: Living with God and Darwin*.

**My friend Carlton.** Carlton Cuse wrote and produced the shows *Lost* and *Bates Motel* and *The Strain* and *Nash Bridges* and *Colony*.

**Jesus taught his disciples a prayer.** The prayer is in the Gospel of Matthew, chapter 6.

**Boredom.** For insight into the relationship between creation and boredom, see Cornelius Plantinga's book *Engaging God's World: A Christian Vision of Faith, Learning, and Living*.

## Part 2. The Blank Page

Stephen King quote is from *On Writing*.

**I once had an idea for a book called *Fire in the Wine*.** That book eventually became *What We Talk About When We Talk About God*. I first came across that line about the fire in the wine in Frederick Bauerschmidt's book *Why the Mystics Matter Now*. The line is from St. Ephraim the Syrian:

> . . . in your Bread is hidden a Spirit not to be eaten,
>   In your Wine dwells a Fire not to be drunk . . .

**Like a tape that's jammed on "repeat."** For more on the tapes that play in our heads, see my RobCast Episode 7, "Changing the Tapes," at robbell.com.

***What is that to you?*** The story about Jesus and Peter is in the Gospel of John, chapter 21.

**. . . the movie *Comedian*.** After Jerry Seinfeld finished making his show *Seinfeld*, he surprised audiences by going onstage late at night in comedy clubs, trying out new material. A camera crew followed him as he created an entirely new act.

**Bruce Springsteen.** One of the best books about Bruce Springsteen is Peter Ames Carlin's book *Bruce*.

**"You" hasn't been attempted before.** Elizabeth Gilbert writes about this in her marvelous book *Big Magic: Creative Living Beyond Fear*.

**Who *am'n't* I?** There's actually a song by the band Mogwai called "Moses? I Amn't." As you can see, they spell it differently.

## Part 3. The Japanese Have a Word for It

Kanye West quote is from Twitter.

**. . . we make our way in the world by the sweat of our brow.** See Genesis 3:19.

**. . . we're all a piece of work.** That's a reference to a line in the letter to the Ephesians (chapter 2) in the New Testament where the Apostle Paul writes, "We're all God's handiwork."

## Part 4. The Thing About Craft

Carlton Cuse quote is from Variety.com's October 27, 2015, article "For Carlton Cuse, Collaboration Is the Key to Creativity" by Debra Birnbaum.

**I once had an idea for a tour.** That tour was in 2006 and it was called "Everything Is Spiritual." We made a film of it that you can get at robbell.com.

**Scottish schoolmaster.** Edwin Abbott is his name, and the book is called *Flatland*.

**. . . my friend Zach.** Zach is the drummer in Jimmy Eat World. You're a fan, right? If you aren't, I recommend starting with the *Futures* album.

## Part 5. The First Number

Tony Iommi quote is from *Iron Man*.

**I once had an idea for a novel.** The book is called *Millones Cajones* and you can get it at robbell.com.

**Eddie.** Eddie started a company that makes a product called Kung Fu Tonic. Google it. Or go to kungfutonic on Instagram to see that legendary Eddie smile.

**I once had an idea for a short film.** We made twenty-four of those short films; they're called Noomas.

## Part 6. The Dickie Factor

Rumi quote is from *Rumi: The Big Red Book*.

**. . . where the waters run deep.** See Proverbs 20:5.

## Part 7. The Two Things You Always Do

Chris Martin quote is from "A Look at the 'Mystery' of Coldplay," *60 Minutes*.

**You first talk to whoever will listen.** I once had an idea for a sermon that involved lots of large exercise balls. It struck me how in the Genesis poem that begins the Bible, the light that comes from the sun and stars is something different from the divine light that emanates from God and guides us into authentic living. You can be in a very dark room but living in the light, and you can be in a well-lit room and yet still be in the dark.

Or something like that.

I found this insight terribly thrilling and decided to build a sermon around it. The room I was preaching in had the stage in the middle and the seats in a series of concentric circles around it. We fastened hooks to the ceiling and I began the sermon by handing out giant exercise balls that represented the different planets and then I asked people to stand on their chairs and attach them to the hooks. I had the balls placed in such a way that the room became a model of the solar system. Then we dimmed the lights and played "Stayin' Alive" from the *Saturday Night Fever* soundtrack while a disco ball was lowered down from the ceiling that represented— you guessed it—the sun.

At this point you might be wondering, *You began a sermon by building a model of the solar system using exercise balls and a disco ball . . . what kind of sermon was this?*

If you are wondering that, you, my friend, are asking an excellent question.

From there I talked about light and transparency and honesty and then I brought the whole thing to what I was convinced would be a compelling crescendo about telling the truth and refusing to live in the dark. I had the lights dimmed around the perimeter of the room so that only the center was full of bright light to illustrate my point . . . my point that no one seemed to get.

I was so convinced that by the end there would be—

I don't know, actually, what I was expecting.

Have you experienced this? You're let down because something you'd been working toward didn't turn out how you wanted it to, but when you reflect on what exactly it was that you were expecting would happen, you can't really articulate it.

I remember finishing the sermon and it was so quiet. And a room with thousands of quiet people in it is . . . quiet. It's a loud kind of quiet. Not the good kind of quiet that comes from deep introspection and meditation and thoughtfulness.

The other kind of quiet. Like the air had been sucked out of the room.

I call it *crickets quiet*.

I had such high hopes for that sermon, and afterward I don't think one person said anything about it.

I bombed,

and I knew it.

You may be true to your ikigai, giving it everything you have, throwing yourself into your work and your path with everything you've got and it may go really well.

Or it may not.

People may sign up, buy, listen, learn, invest, read, register, get involved—or they may not. People may get it. Or they may not.

They may be moved and inspired and compelled, or they may turn to the people next to them when it's done and say, *Where do you want to go for lunch?*

**You do not want to leave me too.** John 6:66–67.

**Aren't we right?** John 8:48.

**Are you betraying me?** Luke 22:48.

**. . . some doubted.** Matthew 28:17.

**Peter-the-caffeinated-disciple protests, No never!** Matthew 16:22.

## Part 8. The Power of the Plates

Robert Irwin quote is from *Seeing Is Forgetting the Name of the Thing One Sees*.

... **how you do anything is how you do everything.** My friend Dan Klyn said this.

... *just in case you might need them someday.* I interviewed The Minimalists for RobCast Episode 15 and they shared an incredibly helpful idea involving the things we keep around *just in case.* You can listen at robbell.com.

**Rhythm.** For more on this, see RobCast Episode 23, "The Cellular Exodus," at robbell.com.

... **this one day that is not like the others is called the Sabbath.** The best book on the Sabbath is *The Sabbath: Its Meaning for Modern Man* (1951) by Abraham Joshua Heschel.

## Part 9. The Exploding Burrito

Abraham Joshua Heschel quote is from *God in Search of Man.*

... **how to be fully present in this moment.** My friend Richard Rohr has a mantra he repeats often: *Just this.*

When you find yourself overwhelmed with all that is coming at you, take a deep breath and say to yourself,

*Just this.*

Just this conversation, just this 1, just this moment. You're building muscle, learning to focus on the 1 in any situation.

My friend Pete Holmes often asks,

*What is lacking in this moment?*

Because the answer is usually "nothing." When you stress that you're missing out, that something terrible and ominous is coming your way because of something you did or didn't do, when you're anxious about some upcoming event, stop. Breathe. Ask yourself,

*What is lacking in this moment?*

Look around you. Remember that the first word about you is *gift*. Some things you can control, some you can't. Do the next right thing, surrender the rest.

I often ask myself,

*What is the next right thing?*

Because that's all you can do. The next right thing. You cannot do it all. You can only do the next right thing in front of you.

**You doing a few things well is a thousand times better than you doing lots and lots of things with half a heart because you're rushing from thing to thing.**

# Acknowledgments

**A thousand thanks to**

Stratton Glaze for all the help, including rescuing me from September, October, and November. Haha.

Mark Baas at Baas Creative for the sublime design work.

Chris Ferebee for fifteen years of friendship, wisdom, and literary agenting.

Everybody at HarperOne, from Mickey Maudlin (editing super as always) to Mark Tauber, Laina Adler, Anna Paustenbach, Lisa Zuniga, Suzanne Wickham, Katy Hamilton, Claudia Boutote, and Caitlin Garing.